Branded

Branded

by Ronnie Kray

A TRUE STORY BY
LENNY HAMILTON

Published by John Blake Publishing Ltd, 3 Bramber Court,
2 Bramber Road, London W14 9PB, England

First published in hardback in 2002

ISBN 1 903402 78 6

British Library Cataloguing-in-Publication Data: A catalogue record
for this book is available from the British Library.

Design by Envy

Printed and bound in Great Britain by CPD (Wales)

1 3 5 7 9 10 8 6 4 2

Papers used by John Blake Publishing Ltd are natural, recyclable products
made from wood grown in sustainable forests. The manufacturing processes
conform to the environmental regulations of the country of origin

For my daughter Katie

Contents

acknowledgements

I should like to give thanks to some friends:

My friend Dave Keen for all his support and encouragement.

My friend Maggie Stewart for reading and correcting
my work many times.

June Watson for having the patience to type it.

I should like also to remember Ian Hendry, the film star (RIP),
for his persistent enthusiasm and encouragement and for making
me believe that I could write a book at all.

dedications

I should like my book dedicated to my friends:

Mr George Cornell (RIP)
A genuine man

Mr Jack McVitie (RIP)
A good friend

Mr Frank Mitchell (RIP)
A gentle giant

Mr Bill Exley (RIP)
On the Kray firm, and my friend

Mr Harry Abrahams (RIP)
Who was always there for me

I would like to thank Roy Wild for all his help
in putting this book together.

foreword

RONNIE KRAY was gripped by evil that night. He ordered two of his henchmen to hold me while he menacingly paced around the kitchen of the twins' top West End club. He picked up a poker and marched across to the large gas fire. When the poker was almost too hot to handle, he stomped over to where I stood.

Without warning he stabbed my body with the poker. The heat burnt through my jacket and shirt. I felt a sharp pain across my stomach. I was panic-stricken. There was no escape; I couldn't break free. The laughter of several of the dozen Kray firm members standing around had now turned to shock. But nobody voiced a protest, they were all too scared of their self-styled 'Colonel' to lift a finger to help me. They knew that if they went against Ronnie, they would be next in the firing line. That was about the only thing you could predict about this gangster — he would brook no disobedience.

Why was Ron Kray trying to kill me? Although rumours that the twins had already done away with a few men had floated around the East End for years, it had not been confirmed they had actually killed anyone. Was I to become the Krays' first casualty? I couldn't think how I had crossed them to warrant such punishment. I had had brushes with them over many years. That was inevitable as we were about the same age and had grown up in the East End, which was at that time a tight-knit community. Although I was a member of a rival criminal firm, I couldn't think what I had done to deserve such punishment, or even any punishment. These thoughts rushed though my head while Ron pondered his next move. Perhaps he knew it all along; he just wanted to torture me physically and mentally by making me wait.

Suddenly he gripped the poker tight and stabbed me in the left cheek. The pain was immense and unbearable. I could feel the flesh on my cheeks and around my eye melt. My eyebrow was burnt away. The smell was awful, but the pain was much, much worse. Tears welled in my eyes. Ron Kray had blinded me. God, what was the monster going to do next? He stared at me for a while. I was terrified. He showed me no remorse; a gleeful look enveloped his face. He struck me across the cheek again. I shut my eyes, but the pain was intense. He took the poker away from my face. I tried to open my eyes, but only the right one would open. He still had that evil smile. It is an expression I will never forget until the day I die. "I'm going to burn your fucking eyes out," he roared. I was too shocked and scared to utter a word. But someone, thank God, did it for me. "No, Ron, not that!" Someone pleaded from the crowd of watching henchmen. This seemed to change Ron's mind. I never did find out who saved my life. Ron calmly walked away, and as he did he said, "OK, you can go now." The job was done — I left.

Ronnie Kray never walked away from my life. He continued to haunt me until the day he died after being locked away for all those years.

Despite my terrible suffering at his hands, I never intended to go to the police. It was not the done thing and what good would it have done? Everyone knew the Krays had detectives in their pocket. I couldn't take the law into my own hands, although God knows I wanted revenge. I could never get near to Ron. He was always with by one of his brothers, firm henchmen or one of his many young lovers.

1

reggie kray and a young boy

THE 1960s were the best years of my life. Although the pubs shut at 10.30 in the evening there was always a party being held around someone's house on a Saturday night, and it was a come one come all life in those days in the East End. It was a constant round of parties. The chaps would all be suited and booted, and the girls would be dressed up in all their finery with not a hair out of place.

It was whilst I was at one of these parties that I received the shock of my life. Everybody was either drinking or dancing and having a good time, but the evening was getting late, and I went to look for my mate, Harry Abrahams, and his wife Jean, as I was tired and wanted to go home.

Someone had told me that Harry had taken Jean upstairs

to lie down as she didn't feel too well, so I went up to see if I could be of any help. On opening the second door I had the fright of my life. There in full view was Reggie Kray with a young boy bent over the bed. Reggie having sex with him. I was so shocked at what I was witnessing I just stood there with my whole body numb and frozen to the spot. I just could not move. Reggie withdrew his penis from the boy and still with a full erection grabbed me by the throat and said, "If you breathe a word to anybody you will be fucking dead and disappear from the face of this earth."

I left the party in a state of shock. I kept saying to myself No! It was Ronnie not Reggie because we all knew Ronnie was gay but in my heart I knew it was Reggie. The next day I went to the Three Crowns pub in Mile End Road and everyone was talking about the fight that went on outside the house where the party had been. I was told that it was the Kray twins knocking hell out of each other. I've often wondered if it could have been over what I had seen the previous night. I heeded Reggie's warning and kept my mouth shut and never mentioned the incident to a living soul.

My friends Harry and Jean Abrahams went to their graves not knowing the truth about Reggie Kray or what went on that fearful night. Some thirty years had passed before I told Ronnie Bender that Reggie was gay or bisexual and of course he did not believe me. I also told Bertie Hook, another good pal of mine of thirty years, that Reggie was gay and he too found it hard to believe, so I never ever spoke about it again.

It was not until Reggie Kray was told that he had cancer and by now had spent thirty-two years of his life in prison that he openly admitted to the Sunday People newspaper that he was bisexual and that he only "came out" because he did not want anyone to blackmail him. I've often wondered if he was pointing the finger at me. If so, there was no need for him to worry, a blackmailer I never have or ever will be.

I am so glad that the Krays are no longer on this earth because in their time, they have caused so much pain and misery to so many decent people and ruined so many lives. How so many people can feel sorry for them is beyond me. They were nothing more than two wicked and evil bastards, and I feel sure Vlad the Impaler could have taken lessons from them. Now they are in the best place for them — six feet under.

The one person I do feel sorry for is Reggie Kray's son. He must be about forty five years old now, and I have been told that he is a very nice person and hardworking, totally unlike his infamous father. He can never be held accountable for the sins of his father, and I would seize this opportunity to wish him a long and healthy life. This I sincerely mean from the bottom of my heart.

2

early
east end
life

I WAS born on the 14th September 1931, in the heart of the East End, near Commercial Road in Stepney. My mother was Jewish — her family originated from Eastern Europe and my father hailed from a family of Scottish farmers. My father first clapped eyes on his future wife when she was peering into a hat shop in the East End. It was love at first sight and he boldly asked her out.

At the time of my birth, the East End had a large Jewish population, and it was a vibrant, exciting place to grow up with many special characters adding to the unique nature of the East End.

Most of the Jews have moved out to North London or Essex now. Relatively few remain in the old heartland. I still live in Bow, but the East End and its different nature from the rest of London has disappeared. So many East Enders have left the area, which has seen the rise in recent years of a large Bangladeshi community centred around the old Kray haunts of Bethnal Green and Whitechapel. The docklands area is now transformed into a gleaming new city full of office workers transported via the modern Docklands Light Railway.

Nearly a third of today's population of Tower Hamlets is of Bangladeshi origin, but when I was growing up in the East End there were hardly any non-white people living in the area. When we saw a black face — it was usually a seaman stopping for a short while at the London Docks — we were amazed. We used to follow these exotic creatures around for miles. All the kids would follow the coloured people, but would never say a word; we just gawped.

The most famous black man in the East End in those days was Prince Monolulu, who was a racing tipster. With his large physique and feathered head-dress, he would have stood out whatever his colour. But because he was black, he became an unmistakable and unmissable figure busy working the crowds down Petticoat Lane.

The idea of million-pound homes in Limehouse was never dreamt of when I was a child in the East End. Stepney and the surrounding district were full of small terraced houses and tenements. We lived at 25 Ely Terrace, a narrow turning off the busy White Horse Lane. Ely Terrace is not there now, as it was bombed out of existence during the Second World War. My mother was easy-going, but my father was very strict. My family of four brothers and three sisters had to do what we were told or we would be in big trouble. All that firm discipline probably did my brothers and sisters a lot of good; it was only me who turned away from the straight and narrow. We also lived among a mainly Jewish community that was quite poor, but friendly enough. People did help each other out then, and there was a real sense of community, which has sadly disappeared and will never be seen again.

My father enjoyed his work, running stables with his father in the Old Ford Road, Bow. They used to hire out the horses and carts to rag-and-bone men.

I had a happy childhood, often playing on the streets with my friends. We were quite poor, and I was at a young age when I first tried to make a few bob. When I was seven years old, I used to go to an egg factory on the corner of our street with some mates of the same age and collect the old wooden egg boxes and cheese boxes and chop them up to make wood bundles, which we sold door to door as firewood for two pence a bundle. There was a Jewish man who had a shed in our street. He used to pull his barrow every Sunday morning to Petticoat Lane in Whitechapel with barrels of Hamisher cucumbers and slated cucumbers on board. My friends and I waited for him to come home from the market as the route to his shed included a steep slope. As he slowly came into the turning, we would get behind his barrow and give him a push. For our assistance he would gratefully give us a cucumber each.

There was another Jewish chap, Jack, who used to push a barrow round our street, selling tin kettles, pots, pans and saucepans. Jack used to wear an old flat cap, his teeth were all rotten and he always had a lighted fag in his mouth.

He used to give us kids some of his goods, and we would knock on doors near our home trying to sell them. For every article we sold, he gave us a commission and we made a few pennies from our endeavours. We nicknamed him 'Put 'em down' because all the women used to crowd around his barrow and when he wasn't looking they would walk away with a kettle, saucepan or whatever they needed indoors. He must have got a bit wise to that because he used to make the women line up and if he saw any of them pick up any of his goods he would shout out, "Now, ladies, put 'em down!"

Because the East End had such a large Jewish population, it was at the centre of the battle in Britain between the fascists and their opponents.

I witnessed Sir Oswald Mosley and his army of blackshirts come marching around our street with their big sticks, smashing the windows of the Jewish houses. I saw fights break out among the Communist Party supporters and the fascists. Most people know about the Battle of Cable Street in 1936, when Mosley and his followers were stopped by the police from holding a large march through the East End streets, because a large counter-demonstration had been organised at the same time. Not many people are aware that Mosley and his mob continued to make their presence felt in the area during the next few years until war broke out.

3

the hurdy—gurdy man

BEFORE THE WAR, a man used to go around the streets with his horse and cart. On the back of the cart he had a roundabout. We would give him an empty jam jar and for that he would give us a ride. In those days, the kids made their own enjoyment by playing street games.

We couldn't afford to buy a scooter in those days, so we made our own out of some wood and ball-bearing wheels. The girls would play hop-scotch on the pavement and do their skipping. Monday morning, the women used to go to the pawnshop to hock their husband's clothes and even their shoes and anything that would fetch a couple of bob. They would be back there early Saturday morning to redeem them just in case their husbands wanted to go out at the weekend. My dad used to go down Club Row on a Sunday morning and buy a piece of leather to mend our shoes and boots, and he would also cut our hair. We couldn't afford to go to the barbers or the cobblers. I used to wear a pair of old black rubbers through the week. When you got a hole in the soles, Dad would cut a piece of cardboard to size and fix it in your rubbers to stop the stones from cutting your feet. My poor old mum would be out in the yard doing her washing in a tin bath with a scrubbing board. In those days everything was done by hand; they didn't have all the electrical appliances that you have today. The same bath that my mother used for the laundry would be used by us all to have our Saturday-night bath in. When all was finished, the bath was hung on the wall in the yard.

Being a big family, when we went to bed we used to sleep two up and two down in a bed. We were brought up on bread and dripping and slices of bread and jam. Christmas time was a treat — we had chicken for dinner, but the only toys that we got were from the Church Mission. In the years of the 1930s, families in the East End could only afford one good square meal a week, which was a lovely roast dinner. When my mother had finished cooking the cabbage, she drained off the green water and Dad would give us all a cupful to drink, saying that it was good for your blood.

We were poor but I think that people were much happier in those days. In the summer the people used to sit outside their houses in the street watching the kids playing. My old nan used to call me over whilst she was sitting there with her black apron on and give me some money and a jug and send me off to the sales bar in the pub to get her a jug of stout. On the way back, I would have a swig and when I got back to her, she would look at me and say, "I hope you have not been drinking my stout on the way back."

And I would reply, "Who me, Nan? Not on your nellie." She would then say, "Well, what's that brown foam doing around your mouth then?" And she would burst out laughing.

There were no school meals in those days. For tuppence ha'penny you could get pie and mash at the pie shop. A man used to come round on a bike with strings of Spanish onions to sell, and then there was a little Jewish bloke with his barrow selling bagels — a round type of bread roll with a hole in the middle. In the winter, you would see the chimney sweeps with their long brushes slung over their shoulders, going round the houses to clean the soot out of the chimneys. There were no betting shops in those days, the bookmakers used to stand out in the streets taking their bets. When a copper came, they would immediately turn around and scarper for all their worth. The coalman would come round with his horse and cart, dropping off bags of coal or coke — most of the people would have it on tick.

People in the East End made their own enjoyment and amusement in those days. They would either listen to the wireless or have some friends round to play cards. Nevertheless everybody enjoyed themselves. On Saturday mornings we would usually go to the pictures. All that cost was one penny so we called it the penny winkles. The Jewish people had their soup kitchens, and if you were that hard up, you could go in them and get a free meal. In those days, to travel anywhere you had to get on a tram that would go along in the centre of the road on the tramlines. When the tram got to its final destination it was turned round on a big turntable so it could start its journey back. The better-off people used to travel about by a horse-drawn cab. You would see the driver sitting there with his long whip in his hand, all spruced up and looking very dignified. Of course, there wasn't so much traffic about in those days. Not like today with cars parked along every turning causing traffic hold-ups.

I am 70 years old this year, and still look back on the days before the Second World War as the good old days. In those days you had more respect towards the elderly people. Not like today, people shooting and carving up people, a lot of it caused by the amount of illegal drugs that are available on our streets today. It is not just in London, but all over the country.

It is silly to say that if the Krays had been around on the streets today, this would not be happening. Of course that is absolute rubbish. But this sort of thing is said, quite obviously by people who did not even know them and are just jumping on the bandwagon, wanting to make a name for themselves.

To me, the Krays were just two very evil men. At least what I am saying is honest. I'm not two-faced like a lot of people are.

As we were a large family we had to take turns to have our meals. The oldest in the family would sit down and have theirs first and so on. My dad would never leave the dinner table until we had all finished our dinner. The bones that were left over from the Sunday joint would be our dinner for the following day. My mum would use them to make a stew for us all, which was very nourishing.

During that period, the women would go to the local butchers and buy a couple of pence worth of bacon bones to make stew. If you had a dog the butcher would give you a bag of rib bones for him. Today, they would call these spare ribs. We also used to go to the local baker's shop and buy a penny bag of broken biscuits and any bread that they had over from the day before. He would give us some bread, which we would take home to our mother and she would make a bread pudding from it.

The East End was a lovely place to live in those days. The old East Enders used to help one another. For instance, if one of the neighbours didn't have enough money to pay their rent when the rent man came around to collect it, the neighbours would chip in and pay it for them. The community in the East End was very tight knit and you could suss when there was a stranger about who didn't come from there. The man of the house in those days was the 'governor', and his word was law. The women were always second best, and they used to say that 'a man was the king of his castle'. But not so today; the women are now on equal rights and quite rightly so. Women are the mainstay of any family and what would this great old country of ours have done without them when the Second World War began? They did their bit as well as any man.

As I look back over the years, with my memories of the old East End, I know that those times have gone forever and I know in my heart that the East End will never be the same again. As the true old cockneys say, 'Gone are the good old days.' Gone are most of the little tenement houses where your neighbours used to talk to one another over their back yards. Today we have high-rise flats, and when people go in and shut their doors that's it. I say it's like living in rabbit hutches. The ones I feel sorry for today are the young children. What have they got to look forward to? The schools are overcrowded, the hospitals are overcrowded and you are lucky if you can get a bed in them now when you are really ill. People lying in the corridors for hours, just waiting to get a bed in one of the wards, and waiting months or years to have that operation that they so badly need. It's all right for the well-off — they can pay and go private and be seen to right away. It's all right for these politicians to tell you what you can live on as they sit in their large country homes away from all the misery that is going on today, eating out in their swanky restaurants, having the finest of foods, and downing expensive wines.

Yes, it's easy to tell the people what they can and can't do as long as it is not happening to them. That is why when I was robbing these large country homes in the 1960s it made me feel good, because to me I was only stealing from a load of hypocrites. Each job that I did, it made me feel great to be able to take a bit off them. For all those crimes that I committed on my own, not once did I get caught by the police. I have always told the truth and, by my own admission, I was never a saint. Not like the Kray twins, who were out to let people think that they were some kind of saints or heroes.

Most people were poor in those days in the East End, but it didn't matter how poor you were — everybody helped everybody else. There really was a sense of community with people mucking in together.

You never heard about the mugging of old people because the elderly were respected then. We opened our street doors just by pulling a string, and the streets were safe to walk in. This, of course, was well before the time the Kray twins supposedly 'ruled' the East End. I have often heard ill-informed people claim the twins kept the streets safe for women and old folk. But the streets of Bethnal Green and Whitechapel were safe for a long time before the Krays were around.

4

evacuation

MY ENJOYABLE childhood was rudely interrupted when I was eight years old by the beginning of the Second World War in 1939.

One day in August my parents were told that I would have to meet all the other children outside our Trafalgar Square School in Stepney, because we were going to be evacuated to the country for safety. I had never travelled outside the East End, let alone to the country before, and for the first time in my life I was scared. I didn't want to leave my mum. I really loved her; she was the best friend I ever had. Nevertheless, we were all lined up outside the school.

My sister Lily and I were the only two from our family who were evacuated, the others being too old. With name labels pinned to us, our gas masks draped over our shoulders, we were lined up by a row of coaches. None of us knew where we were going or what was in store for us. They started loading us onto the coaches and after a quick, emotional goodbye, we were off.

As the coach was trundling along, they told us where we were going. It was to a country village called Eton Wick. For someone who had lived in the East End all his short life, it could have been the other side of the globe for all I knew. All I remember saying to my sister was, "God knows what is going to happen to us."

We finally reached our destination. It had seemed like hours; in fact it had only been two. We were all given a cup of tea and a sandwich. We were split into two groups. I said I wanted to stay with my sister, but they replied that we had to do as we were told. So my sister went into one group and I went into the other. Then we were marched around the village like sheep to be 'picked out' by our foster parents as the evacuation officials knocked on doors. The residents would look us up and down and pick who they wanted. This went on all day and into the night. After the coach ride and walking around all day, I was worn out. Not knowing where my sister was made it so much worse.

In my group I was the only one left. No one wanted me so I was taken back to the hall. The people in charge of the operation were there and saw that I was the only child not to get a billet. The village mayor came in and said there was a couple willing to take me in. So off I went again. We arrived at a small cottage and I was told that this was where I was going to live. A young woman answered the knock on the front door.

I was introduced to her, she signed a paper and I was shown inside.

She said, "My name is Edie Thorton and I am going to be your mother."

I looked at her. She was a hard-looking woman with a hump on her back and I told her quite frankly, "I might have to live here, but you will never be my mother."

I could tell she did not like that. Mrs Thorton told me to take all my clothes off as I was going to have a bath and she was going to bathe me.

I trooped off to the bathroom and locked the door. She came up the stairs and knocked on the door demanding I let her in.

I told her I could bathe myself and she shouted back, "You wait till my husband comes home. He will deal with you, you little guttersnipe."

"I am not a guttersnipe," I replied. "I did not ask if I could come and live here and, by the way, you are getting paid for me while I'm here so if you want me to go I will, right now."

I finished my bath and went downstairs.

Just then the door opened and a tall man came in.

"Hello there," he said. "Who are you?"

I replied, "My name is Lenny, and I'm from London."

Conversation, such as it was, stopped and we sat at the table. He told me he had just finished work at an aircraft factory at a place called Langley.

"It must feel strange living in the country after living in London," Mr Thorton said.

"Yes," I replied, "and I miss me mum and dad and my brothers and sisters."

It was then his wife came in and gave him his dinner. Then she put hers on the table. It looked and smelt so lovely, I just couldn't wait until she brought mine.

Theirs consisted of roast meat, baked potatoes and greens from their own allotment.

All I could do was sit and wait. She brought in a glass of milk and a sandwich.

Her husband said, "Well we've got ours. Where is his?"

Mrs Thorton's reply was brutally frank. "I can't give him anything until I receive his ration book."

It was a very clean home and I was given my chores to do each day. They had their meals, but all I got was sandwiches. I wrote to my mum asking her to take me home, informing her that a dog got better treatment than I did. It was a few months later in mid-November 1939 when my mum and dad came down to see us. They visited my sister, and I am glad to say she had been luckier than I had. She was staying in a good home and living with people who really cared. My mum came to see me and as soon as she set eyes on my miserable appearance she cried, "Oh God! What has happened to you?" I had lost so much weight during my short stay in the country.

"Don't worry, Mum," I said. "I'm OK."

My foster mother, Mrs Thorton, was so nice to me while

my parents were there, but she quickly changed when they went back to London. My mum and dad had left me all new warm clothes and boots for the winter, but as I kissed my mum goodbye and then my dad, I could not tell them how desperately I wanted to travel back to London with them.

As soon as my parents had gone my foster mother said, "I will put these clothes away and you will only wear them when I say so." So much for her changed attitude. I was choked because I knew what my parents had to go without to buy the new clothes for my sister and me.

One night I was told to go to bed early because my foster mother was having some of her family round. I lay in bed thinking of my parents and what they were doing. Finally I fell into slumber. But my misery in the 'idyllic' countryside continued.

My foster parents used to lock me in a cupboard and beat me with a belt when they considered I had been naughty, however unimportant the 'crime'. I soon realised they did not want me in their home at all. All they wanted was the money from the authorities for being a foster parent.

Edie Thorton received money from the Government as well as my ration book, and the food I had wasn't too bad. Still, I was glad when the summer came because when she cut my food down, I could go to her husband's allotment and dig up come carrots to eat. One day I was stealing carrots, and one of the local men saw me and reported the incident to Mrs Thorton. Well, the way she went off, you would have thought I had stolen the crown jewels. When her husband arrived home she told him what I had done; he went mad and hit me with his belt. I told her that if she fed me properly I would have no reason to steal her carrots. She sent for the village MP and the local policeman and they were having thoughts about sending me to a kids' home. That's when my time at her house came to an end, and I was extremely glad to get away from there. They were really not very nice people.

After about nine months they had had enough, and I was taken out of their care and given new foster parents whose surname was Cox. Mrs Cox was a very dear and lovely lady, and her husband was a gentleman. She really looked after me, clothed and fed me well. Each night after supper there was always a bar of chocolate for me. I couldn't have wished for a nicer couple to live with. God bless them both.

The village where we had been staying, Eton Wick, was a lovely village situated about two miles from Windsor Castle and one mile from Eton College. In the winter the Londoners would make snowballs and we would have fun knocking the college boys' hats off, but it was in good fun and taken with good humour.

The people in the village never liked us interlopers, who they called the Londoners. Anything untoward that happened in the village was all down to the Londoners.

My idyllic time in Mrs Cox's lovely little cottage in Alma Road, Eton Wick, seemed to pass by really quickly and I soon found myself back in London with my beloved parents. In the middle of the village there was a large orchard called The Weatbucks, with a lovely old country house in its grounds. It had a big high fence all the way around it to keep prying eyes out. David Niven, the film star, had moved there. Mind you, I didn't ever see him. At the other end of the village was Dorney Common. The army had anti-aircraft guns spread out all over the common. Occasionally they would fire at the German planes that were passing over to drop their bombs on London. One night, a German plane did drop some incendiary bombs and one got lodged in the ceiling of a cottage in Shepherds Walk. It was lucky that the bomb never went off, as it would have burnt the house down. The local villagers were paying thruppence a time to go in and see it. That was the first and last bit of excitement that was to occur in the village during World War II.

By now the locals were beginning to accept the Londoners, and me and my mate Dicky Moughton went and joined the church choir.

My mum and dad came to stay in Eton Wick, to get away from the air raids. They took half of a house opposite where I was staying. I was so glad that they did. My dad got a job in the aircraft factory in Slough doing his bit towards the war effort. Things went all right for quite a while but when anything went wrong, they started to blame the Londoners for everything. My dad got us all together and told us to tell our foster parents that we were going back to London that weekend.

I was pleased, but when I told Mrs Cox, she started to cry. I told her I was very lucky to have had the best foster parents in Eton Wick. I liked them very much. During the few years I was with them they treated me like their own son.

5

very hard times

MY FAMILY had moved to a new house in the East End in late 1943, and we were suffering daily air raids. We were back home where we belonged and together, except for three of my brothers who were in the armed forces fighting for king and country.

My dad, a keen pigeon trainer, was happy because the army sent him pigeons to train for their courier service; hopefully they may have saved some lives during the war. We never went back to school in those days. Because of the air raids the streets were our education. We used to spend a lot of our time in air-raid shelters. One time a German plane gunned Burdett Road, Poplar, just around the corner from our home, and I remember being both terrified and fascinated living in my own great adventure.

In 1943 Hitler's bombs blasted us out of our home. Me, my parents and two of my sisters were in an air-raid shelter all night because the German planes were giving the East End a hammering. When the all-clear sounded we came out of the shelter and walked to what was left of our home.

Everybody was having a hard time, but you have got to hand it to the Cockneys — there were still plenty of smiling faces about and no way were they going to let the Germans get them down.

My dad found another house for us to live in, in Single Street off Burdett Road. He had his yard for his pigeons and carried on training them for the army. This was his contribution towards the war effort. All sorts of army personnel came to see my dad, sometimes to bring him some pigeons and other times to take some away.

By 1944 the East End had suffered years of incessant bombing. Now a new, even more horrible danger confronted us – the German pilotless planes or 'doodlebugs' as they were called. Sometimes they would strike with devastating effect without any warning at all.

One particular night we were in the brick shelter opposite our house, and the sky was lit up with searchlights. Suddenly there was a terrible crash. It really frightened the lives out of us. People were shouting, "This is it, we are all going to die!"

Soon an air-raid warden came into our shelter and said, "Don't worry, the big crash you heard was a German plane. It has been shot down and crashed into the bridge in Grove

Road. The Home guard and the police have captured the crew and are marching them to the local nick."

Everyone was cheering. You would have thought the war had ended.

The next morning a wireless report said that a German pilot's plane had crashed on the bridge in Grove Road. In fact, it was a doodlebug.

We suffered the bombing and the doodlebugs, but then we had an even worse nightmare. The Germans started sending over an even more powerful bomb. It was called the V2, and it wreaked havoc in the East End.

By this time my mum had had enough of running to the nearby shelter, which seemed too flimsy to withstand the power of Hitler's bombs. So she got us booked into the underground shelter in Bethnal Green. Every night we used to catch a bus — the 106 — from Bow and go down the shelter for the night.

We slept on bunk beds. They had a canteen down there and also a stage where they put on shows for the people. When you were down there you would never have thought that there was a war raging outside.

One night in March 1943 we were late getting to the shelter. We had got as far as the entrance where there was a big crowd of people standing outside watching the searchlights.

We made our way through the crowd and down the tube. My mum was making our bunk beds up when suddenly we heard a loud noise. It was then that the wardens came down asking everyone for blankets and sheets because there had been a lot of people crushed in a terrible accident outside. Naturally my mother gave the officials all our bedclothes, as did a lot of other people.

We didn't have any sleep that night and it wasn't till early in the morning that we were told what had happened. When we were finally informed we could go home, everybody picked up their belongings and made their way out. When we got to the top of the escalator and reached the stairs, all you could see were parts of clothing, bloodstains and even pieces of earrings — it was horrible.

We went across to Len's café to get a cup of tea and a bite to eat although none of us felt like eating despite our hunger. It was packed in there and everyone was talking about what had happened down in the tube. One of the wardens, whom my dad knew, came over to our table and spoke to my dad. A lot of people had been crushed that night, men, women and children. Someone had shouted out that there was a landmine coming down and everybody had panicked. They said it was a woman with her child who were the first to fall, then people were just falling on top of each other and getting suffocated.

When we went back the next night we were told 173 people had died and many more had been seriously injured in the Bethnal Green tube disaster.

I will never forget when the war ended in 1945. My dad was listening to the news on the wireless. We were out in the street playing hopscotch when my dad came running out into the street and threw his hat into the air, shouting, "It's all over. The war is over. We've gone and done it. We've finally beaten those German bastards."

By this time everybody was in the street shouting and singing 'It's a long way to Tipperary'.

People were cuddling one another, women and kids were crying and even some men shed a few tears. I will remember that day as long as I live.

That week all the neighbours' ration books were collected to ensure that the children had plenty to eat at our street party. Everyone had Union Jack flags hanging out of their windows and the singing and dancing went on all day and all night.

It was a lovely sight to see everybody singing and dancing, kissing and hugging one another, with no more fear of death plunging from the skies.

6

my employment

AT THE AGE of fourteen, I left school and got my first job at Billingsgate Fish Market. I started off as a bike boy for R.A. Forester of Lovatt Lane, delivering fish to pubs and hotels. I worked there for about twelve months. Then I got a better job with Mac Fisheries as a salesman weighing fish, boxing and lacing them up for their customers. I used to start work at 5 a.m. and finish about 11 p.m., but I coped with the hours because I was earning money.

When I was 15 years old, I had my first meeting with someone who was already a well-known face in the East End and who would ultimately meet his fate at the hands of Ronnie Kray. I was on my way home when a fellow stopped me and asked, "Would you like to carry some empty boxes out of this warehouse for me, as my brother hasn't turned up and I am on my own?"

I agreed and we took turns carrying the boxes up the stairs and loading them onto a railway horse and cart.

When the cart was fully loaded he said I had done well, and that he would like to use me from time to time. He always paid me well and every now and then he would give me a few extra bob.

People respected him in the market. He was tough and no one would try to take liberties with him. His name was George Cornell. Many years later he was the man Ronnie Kray shot dead at point-blank range in the Blind Beggar pub in Whitechapel Road, East London.

At the age of eighteen, I was saying goodbye to my family again as I had passed my medical for the army. I was a conscript. I'd got my papers and I was off to Aldershot Army Camp to start my 18 months of national service. At the end of the 10-week training, I was given a 48-hour pass.

When I returned to the East End it seemed as if I had been away for years. When I came out of Mile End Station I felt so proud walking down the street in my uniform. That mood only lasted a few minutes as I saw a few of my old mates and they started taking the mickey.

Our front door was open as it always was. I walked in and my mum was in the kitchen. She looked up and threw her arms around me and never stopped kissing me.

My dad didn't say much. He just looked at me and said, "Well if you can wear a uniform for the King I guess it's only right to say, 'You are a man now.' "

My brothers and sisters came in and treated me with some money.

I felt on top of the world and had a lovely weekend. I saw all my old mates. To my regret, most of them are dead now.

Finally, it was time to go back to camp. My pass was up.

I said goodbye to my family and I was on my way again.

I had got as far as the Mile End Road, when I bumped in to Tiny Bill — so named because he was so big. He was a local villain — always dressed very smartly and with the looks of a film star. He said, "Hi, Len, where you off to in your old monkey suit?"

"I'm going back to camp," I replied.

He told me I had plenty of time and that I should spend my last few hours with my mates. "Len, I'm just going to have an Indian curry. Come with me, I'll treat you to one."

My stomach ruled my head and I said yes.

By now there were about half a dozen of us and we were all off to the restaurant. Some of my mates were already in there and we sat down at a large table.

Tiny said, "Order whatever you want."

So I did.

Tiny called the owner over and told him to take my order and to serve me straight away, because I had to go back to camp. This he did and it was a lovely meal. We sat at the table and had a good old laugh. It was getting late and I pleaded that I really had to go now.

Tiny said, "OK. Don't worry, I'll pay for the meal."

I said thanks and got up to go. As I got close to the door Tiny shouted to the owner, "Ali, he's having it on his toes without paying." Ali stormed out of the kitchen with a big carving knife. I panicked and scampered down the Mile End Road with Ali chasing after me, brandishing the knife. Thankfully I lost Ali and managed to get my train back to camp.

When we were woken up the next morning, we were told to get our kit packed. We were off to Hillsea Barracks in Portsmouth.

We went through more training and I joined the boxing team. I had about four fights, winning them all. I finished the rest of the training and finally I was posted to Corsham Barracks in Wiltshire, which was a great camp.

I joined the boxing team and had a few fights around the RAF camps in Wiltshire. I lost only a couple on points. By this time a new commanding officer had taken over control of the camp. He was a small Jewish man, very strict and hard. The first thing he did was to stop the boxing team getting extra food. So most of us packed it in.

One evening, with only six more weeks of the 18-month stretch to go, I was lying on top of my bed, when Sir Winston Churchill came on the wireless and said they had extended all national service to two years.

I was choked.

Everybody was moaning. My old mate Johnny Keating came to see me. He was in the Pioneer Corps and stated boldly, "I'm not having this."

"Nor am I," I replied.

We waited till lights out and when all was quiet, we went on the trot.

I managed to get back to the East End, but when I saw my mum I felt guilty and told her I was on leave. The next night I got changed and put on my blue-striped suit and left to go dancing. I stood at the 106 bus stop, not knowing that two regimental police had gone to my house dressed in civvies.

My mum answered the door. She thought they were friends of mine and they asked her where I was.

My mum gave them a very helpful reply. "You must have just missed him. If you hurry you will catch him at the 106 bus stop. He's wearing his best blue pin-striped suit."

I was still at the bus stop when a voice behind me said, "Hello, Len. Home on leave?"

I said, "Yes," and turned around to see these two big blokes. This is it, I thought. They got hold of me and told me who they were, as if I didn't know, and frog-marched me back to camp — divine justice.

I was in front of the Commanding Officer the next morning. He gave me 28 days detention, which I did in Colchester Army Prison.

While you are in there they treat you like a dog and try to break your spirit. So I thought, No way are they going to break me. And they never did.

I did my 28 days and on the morning of my release they gave me a cheese sandwich and a thruppenny bit to get a cup of tea on the train back to camp, plus my railway warrant.
I arrived back at the camp sometime in the afternoon.

I reported to the company office and was marched in to see the commanding officer.

He said, "I hope you have learned your lesson. Now I want you to go back to your barracks and clean your kit. And I mean all your kit, and I want to see it all laid out in perfect order."

I was marched back to the barracks. They gave me two cakes of Blanco — that is a khaki colour — and I set about to blanco my kit.

First, I did all my webbing, and then I started on my clothes. I then did my overcoat, my uniforms, and my vest, pants, socks and shirts. All I had left was the pants I had on. A corporal came by and asked me what the hell I was doing. I explained what the CO had said and off he went.

Back came four MPs and took me to the Guardhouse. I was in there for nearly a week before I came up in front of the board where I was given 56 days' detention. The next day I was escorted back to Colchester. One of the staff came up to me and said, "Back already. You only went out last week. You must like it here."

I said I did and he replied, "When you answer me you will call me 'Staff', as all the wardens in here are Staff Sergeants." They really made my life hell for the first six weeks, but I did everything they ordered. I must admit they nearly did break me.

One night they marched me up to the mess office, put me in a room and left me on my own for about an hour. As I sat there I thought, My God, what are they going to do to me now? Well, God certainly showed me.

They shaved all my hair off and made me run round the parade ground with a full pack whilst holding my rifle above my head. They had stripped me to the waist. Thick frost was on the ground and they turned the cold water hoses on me. I knew in my heart that I couldn't take it much longer.

As I sat in that room I was praying to God to watch over me (which he did). Suddenly the door opened and in came two of the biggest Staff Sergeants you could imagine. They sat at my table, gave me a cigarette and told me that in all their time as Staff Sergeants they have never seen anyone take so much punishment and not complain. In fact, they even said that they admired me for taking so much stick, considering I was such a little bloke.

The door opened again and in came one of the kitchen staff with tea and sandwiches for me. They told me that for the rest of my stay there I would work in the kitchen if I behaved myself. My ordeal was over. Hallelujah!

On the day I left I was wished good luck by the staff and as I was on my way out, Tojo, as we nicknamed him because he looked Japanese, shouted, "Good luck. I don't want to see you anymore."

I got back to camp and went in front of the CO. I think he knew what I had gone through. He placed me on the garden party. It was a nice job. I had been on it for about three weeks when I was called to the company office and I was given 14 days' leave.

The rest of my national service thankfully passed without

incident. I had gone into the army for 18 months and finished up doing two-and-a-half years. I have no regrets at all. At least, as my dad said, it made a man of me.

7

a first meeting with the kray twins

IT WAS SHORTLY after the end of my national service that I had my first meeting with the two infamous characters who were to play such an important role in my life in civvy street.

One day I was walking down Burdett Road on my way home from work, when I saw a big bloke fighting with two young boys. I went over to help them, pushing and shouting at the big bloke. The two lads got away. Little did I know he was a CID officer. If looks could kill, I would have met my maker there and then. He held me until a squad car came.

I was handcuffed and taken to Arbour Square police station in Stepney and thrown in a cell. I thought, If this is what you get for being a Good Samaritan, you can forget it.

After a short while the door opened and I was taken into a small room.

"What the bloody hell am I doing here?" I shouted. "I was just trying to stop a fight."

An officer shouted back. "Stop a fight? Those two blokes that got away were the Kray twins on the run from the army."

"Well," I said, reasonably enough, "how was I supposed to know that?"

They asked me if I was working.

I told them I worked down Billingsgate Fish Market, and I had only been out of the army four weeks. With that they went out of the room and when they came back they asked me if I knew the twins and I said "No", though I had heard of their growing reputation as a couple of 'likely lads'. They gave me a caution. I think they knew that, whatever the unfortunate consequences of my actions, I was telling the truth, and they let me go.

A year later my mother died of a heart attack and I felt as if my world had been torn apart. Our house in Single Street wasn't the same without my beloved mum.

Lil and Jean, my two sisters, and I could do nothing right in my dad's eyes after mum passed away. I stuck it for so long, but I finally left home.

A good friend of Mum's took me in. Her name was Annie. She was a lovely woman and treated me just like one of her own even though she already had two sons and two lovely daughters. Her husband, George, had his own business, so I left the fish market and went to work for him. George was a lovely man, who treated and paid me well. His two sons worked for him, and we all got along fine. My life seemed to be sorting itself out quite nicely on the straight and narrow.

But something happened which would lead indirectly to my life of crime. That something was a lovely looking girl who hailed from Poplar in the East End. I was very shy with girls at that time, but Val knocked me for six. I used to pick her up at her house and we would go to the cinema or go dancing. I had been taking her out for about six weeks when one day I knocked on the door and her mother answered it.

"Val is getting ready," she said, "but before you go in, there is something I would like to ask you."

"OK," I replied.

"Is there anything wrong with you?" she asked.

"No, why?" I answered.

"Well," she said, "do you like my daughter?"

"Of course I do," I said.

"Well, Len, I like you, but you have never kissed my daughter. She is worried there might be something wrong with you."

I felt a right fool.

I said I was sorry and explained that I was a bit shy with girls.

Val's mother smiled at my embarrassed explanation, then smilingly showed me into the living room. Val came in and she looked beautiful.

We went dancing that night but I was too embarrassed to

bring up the conversation with her mother. A few months later we got married and life was great. Two lovely children quickly followed. Our first was a girl—we called her Lorraine. A year later came a son. We named him Leonard, after me.

During our seven years together my wife was always moaning about our lack of money and how we could never afford the finer things of life. This is what partly led me into my life of crime. I know it isn't fair to heap all the blame on her as I could have resisted the urge to find easy pickings, but, in all honesty, I can say I would never have gone down that route if I hadn't been married to her.

I got my first taste of prison for stealing a load of carpets from the East India Dock in the East End. I had been to see a man on information that he was a buyer of stolen goods. He told me that it would take a day or two for him to make all the necessary arrangements. I saw him the next day, and he told me to take the load to Kenningall Road, which was over North London way. He told me to wait there with the load of stolen carpets.

I drove the haul to North London and sat in my lorry waiting for the man to turn up. Well, he turned up all right, only he wasn't on his own. He arrived with three other men in a big Humber car. They were the Flying Squad from Scotland Yard. I realised then that he had set me up, the dirty bastard.

I was arrested and taken to the local nick and charged with being in possession of a stolen load. As my wife was expecting our first baby and because I hadn't been in trouble before, the judge gave me bail to appear in court at a later date.

I finally received notice to appear at Thames Magistrates' Court to answer the charge and the judge gave me three months in prison.

I was put down in the cells to await the prison van and finally I was taken to Brixton Prison to serve my sentence. I felt as if my whole world had collapsed around me. I was only 22 years old. The three-month term could have been a life sentence the way I felt then.

8

doing bird

I WAS ALLOCATED a job working in the prison hospital with six other cons. We had our own ward where we slept and we could have a bath whenever we liked. I was given the job of helping to clean offices.

There were two wards. B Ward held the remand prisoners who were waiting to come up on murder charges.

Being a hospital cleaner, I had to take turns to sleep in the wards at night with the screws on duty, just in case they needed any help. The cells on the ground floor only had iron gates, so the screws could keep a close watch on them.

In one of the cells was a Spaniard who was awaiting trial for the murder of a young girl in Brighton. He had strangled her with her own skipping rope.

In prison all he did each day was paint. Because he was on

remand like all the others he was allowed 'in' whatever he wanted. So he had all these special paints and canvasses sent in. He was doing a painting of Prince Philip in all his braid and medals. He said to me that he hoped he could get it finished before he went to trial. He did, and he gave the painting to the prison Governor.

His case came up at Lewes Criminal court — he was found guilty and was hanged for his crime.

After a fortnight inside, I was given the job of making the screws tea and coffee. They had their own room and each had their own locker where their property was kept. We had one screw that was a bit sarcastic and nobody liked him. He moaned at everybody and everything, one of those types of bloke who had to do what his wife told him and never had a kind word for anyone.

He had a go at one of the cons which lost him his job in the hospital. So I decided to get my own back on him. It may have been childish, but at the time it felt like a proper revenge — when I made him his pot of tea, I used to piss in it.

After about a week of carrying out this revenge he barked at me. "Hamilton!"

I thought I had been rumbled. But a smile broke across his face and turning to me he said, "Hamilton, I'll say this for you, you certainly know how to make a good cup of tea."

"Thank you, sir." Then pushing my luck I asked, "Don't you get pissed off with this job at times?"

He said he did and I thought no wonder you do especially

after what you have been drinking for the past week.

I used to have my meals in B Ward. Whilst I was there, the Bullman Brothers were in on remand waiting trial for the murder of their father. He had been a docker from the East End and when he was drunk he used to beat up their mother. I know they loved their mother, and one day, while he was beating her up, the boys snapped and they both hit him with their docker's hooks and killed him. I am glad to say that when they went to the Old Bailey they were found not guilty and it couldn't have happened to two nicer blokes.

I used to sit at the table next to a very polite and smart man. He was in there for putting Canfradin, a drug, in some coconut-ice sweets, which he gave to his secretary. He fancied her and wanted to dope her up so she was more relaxed in his company. It sounded an extreme way to get someone to like you. Unfortunately, he put too much of the drug in the food and the poisoning eventually killed her.

So there he was on a murder charge. A nice man who loved his wife and kids. I felt sorry for him and within a couple of weeks his blond hair was turning grey from the stress and the remorse he so obviously felt. He went to the old Bailey and got eight years. I was glad for him — we all make mistakes in our life. Nobody is perfect, and I am so pleased that he was never hanged.

If he is still alive, and wherever he is, I really do hope that he is in good health and happy.

The one man I really liked was a chap called Wells. He was

there for stabbing a waitress to death in Kingston upon Thames. His case came up at the Old Bailey and he was found guilty. He told the judge that he wanted to hang as he didn't want to spend the rest of his life in prison. Well, he got his wish, but if you were to sit at a table and eat and talk to these people, you would wonder how they could commit these awful crimes, because they seemed so intelligent and such nice people to talk to. But, as they say, it takes all kinds of people to make this world.

I was released from Brixton Prison about June 1954. I got one month's remission for good behaviour, so I only did two months inside. My wife was waiting for me when they let me out. I hadn't expected to see her as she only had a short time to go before our first child was born.

I got a job driving a lorry for a firm on the Isle of Dogs, delivering oil all over the country. My wages were a mere nine pounds and ten shillings a week as drivers were badly paid in those days. My wife gave birth to our beautiful daughter, born on 31st August 1954.

Although my wages were poor I had to stick the job as it was getting near Christmas. I got into work one morning, and my lorry was loaded for deliveries to towns and villages all over Surrey. One of the deliveries was to a really big house there.

I rang the bell a few times and got no answer. I was so desperate for money, I decided to rob the house. I thought it was a doddle as no one seemed to be around. I was unaware that a woman had taken a photo of my lorry and me as I waited outside looking very suspicious. I was arrested that evening and given bail to appear at Couldson Magistrate's just after the New Year. Of course I lost my job, and when I went to court I was given a six-month imprisonment.

I was taken back to Brixton Prison. On the second day I came up in front of the Governor who said with genuine regret, "You are one chap who I thought would never come back to prison again."

He put me to work in the mailbag shop sewing mailbags for the GPO. I had been in there for about a month when I was called up to see the Governor. He said I had done well the last time I was there, and had shown good behaviour since my unfortunate return. He had decided to put me in an outside job working in the officers' mess. I worked in there for about two months and most of the screws were all right. But you always come across a wrong 'un, as I did one morning.

I had just finished cleaning the floor when a big ginger-headed screw came in and kicked my bucket of water all over the floor. Then he said that the floor was filthy and told me to clean it up.

I looked at him and said, "You are a big fellow and you look like a strong chap. You can fucking well clean it up yourself!"

With that he took me back into the prison and I was put on a special Governor's report. The Governor asked me why I did it.

I told him what had happened. but it was no use, as the Governor always believed the screws. He said that I had kicked the bucket over for no apparent reason.

With that I was given seven days' bread and water, loss of privileges and the loss of seven days' remission. When I had done my seven days' 'chokey', I was given the job of landing cleaner. The job consisted of scrubbing the floors on my hands and knees.

The meals in those days consisted of porridge for breakfast, and the midday meal had potatoes full of 'eyes'. For tea there was an eight ounce cob of bread with a little bit of cheese or a piece of meat of some kind and a small round of margarine that didn't even cover a slice of bread.

For supper the screws would come round with some cons with tin baths filled with cocoa. You would finish up with a cup of mud, as the cons called it. And every night you would get a small rock cake. On Sundays only, you would get a roast dinner — well that's what they called it. Prison food was bloody awful. I was released from prison around May 1955, and couldn't wait to get my beautiful daughter in my arms again.

Eventually I got a job driving for a fruit firm in Covent Garden. I used to load up at the docks all over England and deliver to fruit markets all over the country. It was hard work, but the pay was quite good.

My son was born in September 1955, and he was a lovely child. We lived in my mother-in-law's house in Canton Street, Poplar. She was good to us, but she would always interfere when my wife and I had a row. Gradually I could see our marriage was falling apart.

In September 1959, a week after my birthday, I just couldn't stand it anymore and for the children's sake I left. That was the most heart-breaking decision I have had to make in all my life, as I loved my kids very much, and I still do today.

Our marriage had lasted for seven years. We had had our ups and downs just like anyone else. We had lived with her parents, who helped us many times. But our rows were getting worse and it wasn't fair to the children, so I left.

At first I went to live with one of my brothers while I carried on working in the Covent Garden fruit market. I stuck it for a while but the strain of being away from my kids began to tell.

I missed them so much, and finally I packed my job in, left my brother's house, and found myself a furnished room in North London.

The last of my money was nearly gone and I owed the landlord four weeks' rent. I liked him and he liked me and told me not to worry, something would turn up and I could pay off my back rent in instalments.

I went to the East End to work for Yiddle Davis. At the time his was the biggest transport firm in the country. There I saw Yiddle's brother Hubby. I told him I had been a driver on the fruit market and that I knew my way all over the country. I told him I was away from my wife and where I was living.

He asked me a few more questions then he took me out in the yard.

He said, "See that lorry over there. That's got to be in Newcastle by eight o'clock in the morning."

"It'll be there," I said.

He gave me the driving job and I arrived in Newcastle at 6.30 a.m. I went into the works canteen to have something to eat.

When I got back to my lorry the night shift had unloaded it and I was ready to start back home when the manger of the works said he had a full load to get back to London for the docks. It was a good payload, so I took it. The lorry loaded, I grabbed a couple of hours' sleep and just before I left I phoned Hubby and told him what had happened. He was very pleased.

I got home to my room at eight o'clock in the evening. I had a wash and went to bed. I dropped off my load at the docks the next morning. I was back in the yard by 10.30 a.m. I went to see Hubby. He was pleased, and he gave me a better lorry, which I had to drive to Port Talbot in Wales. Now I was earning a decent wage, working long hours to fill up the time to help get over the desperate feeling of missing my children.

I stayed with the firm for about nine months; I was convinced that I was back on the straight and narrow. I had paid my back rent and I was out of trouble.

The work was hard. You earned every penny, but if you were a good worker, then you were looked after. I was tired so I decided to take a week off work. It was during that time that I met a mate of mine. I knew he didn't live life on the straight, but he was a good sort. He always seemed to have plenty of money, and he kept himself to himself and didn't cause a fuss.

We went and had a drink in the Globe pub in Mile End Road. I had my usual — brown ale. We got talking and when I told him what I was doing, he said, "You must be mad. All that work and what do they pay you? Next to nothing. How would you like to earn some easy money?"

The idea was one that appealed, and I was hooked again on easy street. He told me he knew where a lorry was parked, loaded with metal. As he couldn't drive a big lorry he needed a driver. He said we would go 50–50 and he already had a metal dealer to buy the load. It sounded so good, I just couldn't refuse it.

A couple of nights later we went out and got the lorry. I drove it and he followed me in his car. The metal dealer was waiting for us and when the lorry was unloaded, we went to his office. He opened the safe and paid us out in readies, three and a half grand, which we split equally between the two of us.

We dumped the lorry and we went and had a drink.

He said, "Not bad for a few hours' work. Will I be seeing you again?"

"OK," I said, well chuffed with the easy money I had made. We had earned a tidy sum together so I packed in my job thinking, Sod that for a lark.

I treated myself and a mate to a holiday. We went to Jersey for a fortnight and had a lovely time. From then on every time I had a good earner I would pack my bag and be off to Jersey.

Back in the East End I started going to spielers. We used to play rummy and kalooki and I was a very lucky card player.

I used to go to a club in Stamford Hill, The Green Dragon Club in Whitechapel, and also the 81 Club in the Mile End Road. That's where I met one of the best mates I ever had.

9

on harry abrahams' firm

HIS NAME was Harry Abrahams. He was married to a girl named Jean, who became a very good friend to me. I first met Harry in 1960. He was about 25 years old, 5 foot 6 inches tall, and of a stocky build. He had his own firm, which was well known in the East End.

One night I came out of the club in Mile End and across came Harry Abrahams with a few of his firm. We got talking and he said, "How would you like to earn some easy money?"

That phrase, as ever, grabbed my interest. He told me that his firm had done a job in Paddington, but in the rush to get away they had left their getaway car parked in a side street. Now. Harry wanted the getaway vehicle back. It seemed such a waste to him to leave it on the other side of London.

He said he would give me two hundred quid if I retrieved the car for him, as he didn't want any of his firm to go back to the scene of the crime. That was a lot of money in those days so I gladly agreed.

The next day I caught the tube to Paddington and drove the car back to the East End — easy money.

From then on Harry used to take me everywhere with him. He was a good spender, and on many occasions I witnessed him putting his hand into his pocket and giving old folks some money for a treat.

Harry had two daughters at that time and on many occasions I would stay at his house and look after them when he and Jean went out for a drink.

I didn't mind as they were lovely kids and, to be honest, I couldn't take the drink the way they knocked it back. One prominent member of Harry's firm was Albert Donoghue. He was a good-looking chap, tall and well built. He was also a very quiet chap and never spoke out of turn. I got on well with the other members of the team. They all had plenty of money and all enjoyed themselves. Harry liked me as much as I liked him.

Now I was working full-time as Harry's driver. None of his firm were liberty-takers, unlike the Kray firm.

Later when Ronnie Kray branded me with a poker, I believed he had done it to attack Harry. To show him who was the real boss of the East End.

But all good things come to an end eventually, and sometime later Harry was grassed up for robbing a bank in

Hackney. He got five years' imprisonment. When he went away, I felt lost. It was like taking my right arm away.

Much to the amazement of a lot of people, Albert Donoghue went to work for the Krays. We couldn't believe it, especially as he knew what treatment they had meted out to me.

By this time, I was quite flush. I sometimes frequented the East End clubs, but I went up the West End more. I often went to clubs such as the 'Tryol' in Old Compton Street. I would bump into some of the known underworld villains, such as Albert Dimes, then a top man in the West End. Everyone used to call him Big Albert. I liked him, we got on well, and he called me 'Titch'.

Jack Spot was then the guv'nor in the West End and at the racetracks around the south-east of England. He never used to trouble the East End like the Krays started to.

Jack Spot was a nice fella as far as I could see. You can only take people as you find them and he was pleasant to me. He ruled the underworld for many years, but his grip on it was now beginning to loosen as up-and-coming firms battled for supremacy. He had become famous during the Battle of Cable Street, which I had witnessed in 1936. Jack helped lead the fight against the fascists, which earned him a lot of respect in the East End.

10

ronnie's mynah bird

THERE WERE NOW many younger pretenders to the underworld throne. The Krays were one of the new competitors who were advancing at a rapid pace.

I always tried to keep my distance from them, but you couldn't help being aware of their growing influence and notoriety in the East End. You heard stories about their ferocious fighting ability and how they were getting together a powerful firm.

One day in 1960, I was summoned to the Kray's house in Vallance Road, Bethnal Green, where they had been brought up and still lived. Their mother, Mrs Violet Kray, opened the door to me and let me in. She was a lovely person and I liked her. Mrs Kray showed me into a nicely furnished room next to the kitchen. She made me a cup of tea and said Ronnie wouldn't be long. She then went out to do her shopping.

The door that led to the kitchen had a curtain pulled across it. As I sat there I could hear what I thought was Ronnie coughing. Then I heard something going up and down the music scale. It seemed to be coming from behind me, but I just sat there with my cup of tea in my hand. Then a voice started saying, "Ronnie is a gangster. That Ronnie is a gangster. That Ronnie is a gangster."

After a few seconds the chant would start again.

I dropped my cup of tea in shock. Was this some weird psychological experiment designed to freak me out? If it was, it was doing the trick.

The curtain was then drawn back and a ferocious-looking Ronnie Kray appeared half-shaved.

I thought he was coming over to put one on me.

I must say, at that moment my stomach was on the floor and my legs went to jelly. Ronnie had an immense aura about him. He looked terrifying.

With that he went behind me so I jumped up. It was then that he pulled the cover off a large bird case and shouted at its little occupant. "If you don't shut up, I am going to wring your fucking neck."

Then, without saying a word to me, he went back to finish his shave. When he returned he had a smile on his face and he said to me, "What do you think of a fucking bird like that?"

Then he pointed his finger and shouted again, "One day, I am going to wring your fucking neck."

The bird shut up after that. Even it knew when to shut up in Ronnie's presence.

I asked Ronnie what it was, as I had never seen anything like it before. He told me it was an Indian mynah bird.

"The bastard will get me hung one day," he confided.

Ronnie got dressed and I must admit that he did look the part of the gangster boss. He was immaculately dressed just as his brothers Reggie and Charlie always were.

Then he asked, "I suppose you must be wondering why I sent for you?" I meekly nodded. "You go in the Green Dragon and the 81 Club and also Joe Corals, don't you? You play cards in all these spielers, don't you?"

I said I did go to these gambling clubs.

"Do you ever hear anyone talk about us, I mean, you know, slag us off?"

I told him, "No, I have never heard anyone speak about you in that way and that is the truth."

"If you do hear anyone talk about me or my brothers would you let me know?"

"Of course I will," I replied.

He patted me on the back and said, "You're OK."

Before I left he told me not to tell anyone about our little chat and then he told me I could go now. Boy, was I glad to get out of there.

11

jersey

AS WELL AS driving Harry Abrahams around I still did a few jobs of my own. Each time I had a tickle, I would go to Jersey for a couple of weeks to get away from it all. I had some friends who had a guesthouse in St Helier.

While I was there I would spend the days on the beach soaking up the sun, and in the evening, I would drink in the island's many bars and clubs.

I used to go to the Tartan Bar in Corbierre quite a lot and I would frequent a nightclub called The Watersplash in St Owens. It was here that I met the great comedian, Ted Rogers, and topping the bill was a very good-looking girl from the East End. Her name was Vera Day. One night I invited Ted to my table for a drink. He accepted my invitation and afterwards we were invited to a millionaire's home for a party. We all had a lovely time and by the time I left nearly everybody was drunk. Ted had left early, but I stayed till the early hours of the morning.

I had been in Jersey for just over a week by now, and lying out on the beach I was feeling quite relaxed. It was a very hot day, and the beach was full of families enjoying themselves. There were people in the sea with their rubber boats, and the young children were splashing about in the pools left behind when the tide had gone out. It was great to see everyone having a good time.

Suddenly there was a bit of commotion only a short way from where I was lying. It was caused by some men playing football, which didn't seem to me to be that outrageous an activity for a beach. But to my surprise, when I looked up I couldn't believe my eyes. It was Reggie and Ronnie Kray with some of their firm.

I never thought I'd see the day when the twins and their gang were dressed in swimming costumes, noisily enjoying themselves as they kicked the football around.

I couldn't get out of there quick enough.

Making sure they hadn't noticed me, I got my things together and went back to my lodging. I packed my bags as quick as possible and got the next plane out of Jersey.

When I got back to the East End my pal Ken said, "Blimey, you're home early. What's the matter? Weren't you having a good time?" When I told him who I had seen playing on the beach, he said he would have done exactly the same.

12

a few tickles in the sixties

IT WAS AT that time that I had got myself a job working for a firm in the Highway, Stepney. The firm was called Raysil. They dealt in imports and exports of women's clothing. I was the assistant bank foreman at the time, checking the goods in and out of the warehouse.

The governor of the firm was nice man, and very good to me. That is why I felt really terrible involving his firm in the crime that I was going to commit. It was Christmas Eve morning and all the staff were paid off with their holiday money and bonuses. The firm would open again after the New Year. Just before I was leaving, the Governor called me into his office and, as I was living in Stamford Hill, North London at the time and my car was in for repair, he told me that I could take one of the firm's vans home and use it over the Christmas holiday. I thanked him for his kind gesture and took one of the vans home. I had a basement flat in Chardenay Road and parked the van outside. I was getting myself ready to go and meet the young lady whom I was taking out at the time. She lived in Poplar.

I was just about to leave my flat, when my street door bell rang, and there standing before me was my old pal Ken with a friend, so I called them in. I asked them what they wanted as I was just on my way out.

Ken asked me if he could borrow the van as he and his friend Micky had broken into a warehouse in Hackney and had all the goods ready to be collected. Ken said it was their Christmas money and as they were both skint they had no money to buy the kids their Christmas presents.

I told Ken, "If it's money you want I can let you have enough to tide you both over."

Ken thanked me but insisted that he wanted to borrow the van and pick up their bent gear. I told him that I could not lend him the van, but as a favour I would take them back to the warehouse and pick their gear up and deliver it for them to where it had to go free of charge. However, little did they know that when they broke into the warehouse they had set off a delayed burglar alarm. As we pulled up outside the warehouse, which was situated in an alleyway, Micky was in the back of the van and Ken was sitting next to me. As it was a diesel van, we couldn't hear the alarm bells ringing above the noise of the engine. Ken was just about to get out of the van, when I saw a police car coming towards us from the other entrance at the back of the alley. Ken had the cab door open, so I pulled him back and shouted, "Old Bill."

I sped off with the old bill chasing after us. As I turned the corner, Ken jumped out and got away, thank God. By this time, Micky had opened the back door of the van. He picked up the spare wheel and threw it at the police car that was chasing us. It landed on the bonnet of their car but luckily bounced off and went over the car roof. By now I knew that I had no chance of losing them, so I pulled up outside a large estate. I jumped out of the van and ran into the estate with the old bill chasing after me. I shinned up a drainpipe of a block of flats, but by the time I had got to the top, the old bill were already there and had let two big Alsatian dogs loose on me. What could I do but give myself up? Looking at the size of the two dogs and the size of me, they would have devoured me in no time. The police told me to lie face down, with the two dogs standing over me. They came over and handcuffed me behind my back. On the way back to the police car, they started shoving me and giving me a few slaps about the face. Micky was already in the back of a police van, and they just slung me inside. As we were on the way back to Hackney police station, the old bill really laid into Micky for throwing that spare tyre at them. We arrived at Hackney police station and were both thrown into a cell. After a short while the cell door opened and in came some police officers, including the one that had been punching Micky in the back of the van. I really had to admire Micky, because as quick as a flash he jumped up and punched him straight on the chin and knocked him out cold. Micky was a very powerful man, and as the rest of the old bill came into the cell throwing punches at us, Micky was knocking them out cold. They finally restrained us and took us into a room where they charged us with burglary and assaulting police officers. We were then taken back to the cells and banged up until after the Christmas holidays. We never even smelt a Christmas dinner, and they say at that time of the year 'good will to all men'. Hmmm.

After Christmas we were taken to Brixton Prison and held in custody until the date of our trial. After a couple of months in Brixton prison, we were taken to the inner London Sessions for our trial. I must give Micky credit, because even in the dock, he shouted to the judge that he could do what he liked to him, but to let me go free, as I was innocent. The trial lasted nearly a week and Micky wound up getting five years. The judge must have taken some notice of Micky, because I got four years. So much for trying to do a pal a good turn! The only good thing that came out of it all was that Kenny got away with it. But do you know, not once did he come to the nick and visit me, or thank me for taking the rap for him. Still, as they say, that's how the cookie crumbles.

It was while I was serving that term of imprisonment that I decided that when I got out I would work on my own. That way you'd only have yourself to worry about and if you did a job and got away clean, kept your mouth shut and didn't start throwing your money about, who was to know? I got friendly with Alf, who used to get first-class information on properties and what tom foolery they had on the premises. So we struck up a relationship. Alf would give me the information. Then I would do the job and give him a percentage of each robbery I did. After each job he would go back to his world and I mine.

One night I was on one of Alf's jobs in Cheyne Walk off the Chelsea Embankment. I'd climbed the drainpipe and was now on the roof. It was pouring down with rain and the wind was blowing like all hell was let loose. I must have lost my bearings for a bit, but I finally got the window open and went inside. I stood there until my eyes became focused. As I walked to the middle of the room I noticed two single beds. Right away I knew that I was in the wrong room, and there before my very eyes were two young children — fast asleep. They had slept right through the gale that was going on outside. I stepped back into the shadows of the room and went out the same way that I had come in, securing the window behind me.

I met Alf the next day and explained what had happened. I agreed that it was my fault that we had lost a nice little tickle, and offered him some of my own money. He looked at me and smiled, and said if those kids had woken, there was no telling how it would have affected them for the rest of their lives. "Don't worry, Len," he said. "You did the right thing, there will be plenty more to come." And so there was. As time went by the information was getting better and better and the money was rolling in. I had a job to do somewhere in England. I booked myself into a nice hotel and each day I would have a ride out to the premises that I would finally wind up robbing. It had been a week now and I was having a drink in the hotel bar, when one of the barmen started asking me all sorts of questions. So I told him that I was on my holidays and was touring all over England. If you have stayed in hotels, you will know what I mean — some of these barmen are so nosy. The night had come for me to do the job that I came for. Before I left my hotel room I checked to see that all my tools were there. They were, and I packed them away in my holdall. As I left the hotel that cold and windy night, the door porter gave me a nod and had my car brought round for me. Before I left I gave him his regular tip.

"Good night, sir. I wouldn't wish anybody out on a cold night like this," he said.

And I replied, "You would, if you were going to meet who I am."

With that he laughed and said again, "Good night, sir, and good luck."

I am going to need all of that luck before the night is over, I thought. I reached my destination where I was hopefully to pull off this job. I parked my car but not before changing over the number plates, just in case something went wrong. I started on foot through the forest carrying my holdall. I had gone about a mile when I came to the clearing, and there right in front of me was the lovely old mansion.

I made my way to the spot where I could climb onto the roof. I sat up there for some time waiting for everyone to get settled. Then all of a sudden, lights started shining everywhere. Right away I thought, That's it, I'm done for, it must be the police shining their lights all over the mansion.

I edged my way to a corner of the roof and as I peered down into the grounds, to my amazement, all I could see were Rollers, Bentleys and other well-known cars entering the estate. Men and woman were alighting from these beautiful cars, the men in their top hats and tails, and the women in their fabulous ball gowns. It was then that I realised there was a ball going on in this lovely old place. I sat there for an hour or so and decided it was now or never. I let myself in and made my way to the master bedroom passing on my way a long corridor, where there were several statues of men in armour. I finally arrived at the master bedroom. Before I entered I could hear the music coming from the downstairs. My heart was beating a lot faster, and now the adrenaline was flowing quickly through my veins. Once in the bedroom I started to gather up the jewellery. To my surprise they had left the wall safe open, the contents of which I added to my collection. Once I had what I had come for I started to make my escape, my pockets bulging with my ill-gotten gains.

Whilst I was making my way back down the corridor, to my surprise one of the doors opened, and by quick thinking, I hid behind one of the suits of armour. A young couple came out of the room and by the way they were talking, I knew that they had been enjoying the fruits of life. I waited until they had both disappeared out of sight and made my way into the grounds. I got back to my car, had a change of clothes and made my way back to the hotel where I was staying. The same doorman was there when I arrived and had my car parked up for me. As I was entering the hotel he said to me, "Did you have a pleasant evening, sir?"

"Yes, thank you very much," I replied.

With that I took myself up to my bedroom and thought to myself, Yes I have had a very pleasant evening, thank you.

I arrived back in London the following afternoon with my booty. I phoned up Alf and told him that all had gone well and to meet me in Hyde Park. We would take the tom to our buyer and get ourselves a good price. The buyer was a nice Jewish man and a jeweller himself. We arrived at his house and he went through all the gear writing each item down. He finally came to a price of quite a few thousand quid. I agreed to his price and arranged to come and see him the next day as he didn't keep that amount of money in his house. We left the buyer and went to the Hilton Hotel for a bloody good drink.

I arrived at the buyer's house the next day; he had the money ready for me. It took a while, but when I had finished counting it and found it was all there, we shook hands and he wished me luck and I left. I met Alf that evening and gave him his commission.

"Thank you, Len," he said. "Nice doing business with you."
I smiled at him, shook his hand and left. We did a couple

more deals together but sadly Alf had a stroke and passed away. The little Jewish buyer, who was a very fair man, passed away in 1983. Two genuine, nice people, God rest their souls. They don't come any better. As I look back over the years and reminisce about all the things I have done, it is hard to believe that I have climbed up drainpipes forty or fifty feet high when now it is hard for me to climb the stairs to bed, as I suffer from vertigo. Now God must have made me this way for some reason. But I don't know what.

It was another time in the 60s and I was working with another firm. All good boys and good thieves. It was a Saturday morning. We had stolen a heavy goods van and changed the number plates. The job was in the West End of London, its exact location I couldn't say. We were going to steal a load of coats that had just arrived in the country. On good information we knew that there would be no one in the building, so my pal got in and turned off the alarm bells. His job done, the premises were ours for the looting. It took us about two-and-a-half to three hours to load our ill-gotten gains on the vehicle. In all it was about a hundred grand's worth but we would only see a certain amount of that. Whilst my pals were locking the premises up, I was downstairs securing the back doors of the lorry.

All of a sudden a woman's voice shouted out to me. "'Ere! Would you and your mates like a cup of tea?"

When I looked up there was this grand old lady sitting on her veranda, willing to give four crooks a cup of tea.

I said, "Yes please, we'd love some."

When my pals returned to the lorry, having made sure that the premises we had just robbed were secure, I told them that this old lady was bringing us down some tea.

They said, "You must be mad, Len, we just want to get the fuck out of here, and the sooner the better."

With that the old girl appeared with a pot of tea on a tray and some cucumber sandwiches, which we couldn't refuse. As we were drinking our tea and eating the sandwiches, she said, "Michael," — that's what I told her my name was — "do you work for these people?"

"No," I replied, "I have come down from the north to pick these goods up. The men that have loaded me up are something to do with the firm. I'm only the driver."

With that she said; "Do you know, I have been watching them premises for a while now and, as you seem such a nice boy, I have got to tell you that the people who own those premises seem to me to be very seedy people."

And I replied to her, "Ma'am, all I am here for is to clear the place out. I am a driver and have to do what I am told."

I thanked her for the tea and sandwiches and we left.

On the way back when I told the others what she had said, one of them answered, "Well, Len, it just goes to prove that you can't trust anyone nowadays."

13

before
the
branding

BEFORE I was branded by Ronnie Kray, I had had several run-ins with the twins. Growing up in the East End at about the same time as me made it inevitable, I guess. They dominated the manor for years, seemingly all-powerful, untouchable by the rule of law. They ruled by fear with tentacles of their firm pervading every nook and cranny of Bethnal Green, Bow, Whitechapel, Stepney, Wapping and the Isle of Dogs.

Their spies were everywhere — word soon got back to the twins if someone had a nice little 'tickle', and they soon felt the pressure from Reggie and Ronnie's henchmen to give the twins a cut of the proceeds. It was almost like a perversion of the Middle Ages system when everyone was expected to give a tithe or tenth of their earnings to the Church. Now it was the not-so-honest underworld labourers who had to give up a share of their cash to the all-powerful twins. You didn't mess with them — you knew better.

Soon the twins were moving into the West End and mixing with the rich and famous, posing for the now-famous photos with international celebrities and mingling with leading politicians of the day. But pride comes before the fall, as the saying goes, and the Krays started to believe in their own publicity, that they were untouchable.

One thing you don't do is grass on your own — or as the Jewish people used to say, 'stum a crum'. That is one reason why at the time of the Kray trial in 1969, so many people turned against them because, despite the ignorance of this today, the Krays had hurt and robbed their own.

I believe that if the Krays had got their money only from racetracks and the West End of London, leaving the East End alone, they would have become very rich people and might never have served such a long time in prison.

The Krays' two most well-known victims, George Cornell and Jack 'The Hat' McVitie, were both friends of mine. I knew them both for many years. Neither of them lived on the right side of the law, but they never deserved to die in such cold-blooded ways. Ronnie Kray shot George in the Blind Beggar pub in Whitechapel, and Jack was knifed to death by Reggie after he was lured to a supposed party in Stoke Newington.

I gave up life on the straight and narrow for the rich pickings from a life of crime, mainly burglary of upmarket homes. This led to a part-time job working for a notorious East End firm that was a rival to the Krays' own gang. In fact, one of my firm's members, Albert Donoghue, later jumped ship to join the Krays shortly after he had been shot by Reggie Kray because of a row over me.

I am East End born and bred and unlike most I have stayed in the manor. Some of the characters I grew up with have now moved away to create that old East-End community feeling in leafier Essex. Some had no choice in the matter and are serving time at Her Majesty's pleasure, and some have sadly, others not so sadly, passed away.

It has always been an unwritten rule in the East End that you don't hurt your own and you don't rob your own. I may have led a life of crime and I am not particularly proud of some of the things I have done, but I never hurt my own. My criminal targets were the posh countryside and West-End homes of the wealthy. I couldn't live with myself if I had robbed anyone in the East End. The Krays did hurt their own and they paid the price.

I've known the Kray Twins for nearly 50 years. I remember the first club they owned was the Regal Snooker Hall in Eric Street, off the Mile End Road. It was next door to the Mile End Arena that used to stage boxing in the afternoon and wrestling in the evening. When I was a kid, before the Second World War, I saw great fighters there such as Eric Boon and Arthur Danahar. After the war good boxers such as Bobby Ramsey and George Walker appeared there. I remember one evening an American actor Richard Wydmark was there, accompanied by another actor, Mike Mazrki. Mike stepped into the ring and refereed a wrestling match. The old Mile End Arena attracted all sorts of stars who came to see the fights. In those days it was one of the most well-known landmarks in the East End.

The Regal Snooker Hall was once a picture palace. When we were kids we used to go there on Saturday mornings to see old cowboy films such as Hopalong Cassidy and Ken Maynard, and who could forget the Tarzan films with Johnny Weissemuller. It used to cost us one penny to get in.

When the Krays took over the Regal Snooker Hall, many East Enders had a lot of respect for them. Mind you, the twins were coming up in the world and from then on you can chart the rise and eventual fall of the Kray twins.

Not long after the Krays had taken over the Regal Snooker Hall, two friends of mine, Leslie Garrett and Henry Rutter, were making their way into the hall when they were confronted by some blokes who were standing outside. A fight broke out, and Leslie and Henry had a bloody good fight and walked away. Now here we have two honest and hard-working chaps neither of whom had ever been in trouble with the police. Leslie was a boiler coverer and Henry was a painter and decorator. All they were doing was going to have a game of snooker, which they did after the fight. Now, Dicky Moughton was a friend of ours. We were both evacuated to Eton Wick and remained friends until he went to work for the Krays. Dicky and I had some good times together and it puzzled me how he came to work for them. I met Dicky again when we were both serving out prison sentences. I asked him what had made him go and work for the Kray twins, and he told me that if he stayed with them, they would make him a rich man. Well, Dicky passed away from cancer in Whipps Cross Hospital when he was 48 years old. He left a lovely family and, to my knowledge, he never died a rich man. God rest his soul. Anyway, when Leslie and Henry were playing their game of snooker, Dicky went over to them and told them that the Kray twins were on their way over to the hall and that they had better clear off because they were furious with them for having a fight with their friends. Word spread like wildfire that the twins were going to hurt them (meaning cut or shoot them).

Nobody saw Leslie or Henry for a while and this made the twins even more angry. They had their spies out trying to find out if anybody knew where they were. If anybody did know, then it would be a big favour they would be doing the twins to let them know where exactly my mates were. However, like everything else, the longer it went on the less people talked about it. The Krays never did get their hands on them.

It was some years later that I was loading my lorry with Jersey potatoes in Portsmouth Docks, Camber Quay, when my name was called out to back the lorry on the bank ready for loading. Having done this, I was standing by my lorry, ready for the dockers to wheel the sacks of potatoes on their barrows for me to load. As I was loading up, a bloke that was loading the lorry next to mine shouted over to me.

"Hey, don't you talk to us old country bums now?"

And to my amazement it was good old Henry Rutter. I got loaded, roped and sheeted and then met Henry and Leslie in the cafe on the dockside.

We had a good chat about the old times and they both told me how they had got their jobs in the docks. They asked me what was going on up in London and to put their minds at rest. I told them that the twins were really after them at that time and that Dicky had said to me that if I were to see you, you were both to stay away, because the twins never forget. I told the pair of them I would not tell a living soul that I had seen them and I never have, until now.

The Krays did them a big favour in a way because they both got good honest jobs after that. Henry got his job on the docks first and then he got Leslie a job there too. It was hard work but now Leslie had met a nice girl, and they were both saving up their hard-earned money so they could buy a pub. Henry had met a lovely woman and they were both very happy and told me that they would never go back to London again.

As I was driving back to London with my load of potatoes for delivery to Covent Garden, I couldn't help thinking about the two of them, and was so pleased they were doing well. I never did mention to anyone that I had seen them, for I knew that if the Krays knew where they were, they would have been down to Portsmouth to do more of their evil deeds.

It was some months later that I was back down in Portsmouth for another load. Leslie and Henry were still working there. I was unable to get loaded that day, so it meant that I had to stay overnight. Leslie took me back to his young lady's house and her mother told me to stay the night, so I did. They sent out for some faggots at the local takeaway, and I must say that I really enjoyed the meal — it was the first time I had had faggots in a long, long time.

Leslie's young lady and her mother went to bed, and Leslie and I sat there reminiscing about the old days. We finally went to bed. When I woke the next morning, his young lady had cooked us a lovely breakfast. I thanked her and her mother for their hospitality, but they would not take a single penny from me.

We said our goodbyes and I gave Leslie a lift to the docks. After a few hours I was loaded and said goodbye to Leslie and Henry, not knowing that that was the last time I would be seeing them.

Leslie did buy a pub, in fact he bought three, and bought a lovely house in Hayling Island. I am sorry to say that Leslie has since passed away. And Henry? Well, I haven't got a clue where he is or if he is still living. If he is alive, I want him to know that I haven't forgotten him and may God bless him.

So here were two hard-working men that had to leave London for fear of the Kray twins, and we all know how fear can affect people. That was how the Krays ruled the East End of London for so long.

The next club the Krays owned was the Double R drinking club, which was a big old house in Bow Road. Reggie opened it while Ronnie was in prison. I must say that Reggie did have class and I think the Double R was the smartest club ever to be seen in the East End.

A lot of people liked Reggie in those days, because, unlike Ronnie, you could talk to him. By now the Kray firm was getting bigger and it attracted a lot of hangers-on. The Krays had opened the Kentucky Club in Mile End Road, another very smart club. You had to give it to them — they did have style. By now they had their long-term fraud firms going for them and were pulling in the cash. Plus they had their protection rackets that were bringing in plenty of money. I must admit that then even I wished good luck to them. It was good to see a couple of East End boys doing well.

With plenty of money coming in, they always dressed immaculately. Even with all they had, they wanted more — they wanted power. They had a lot of bent Old Bill on their books, who would help them for a fee.

Ronnie was subject to bad moods, and to show their strength, the twins were cutting and carving people up in the East End — even shooting them.

One time, my mate Roy Wild and I were having a drink in The Rupert Club, Rupert Street near Shaftesbury Avenue, owned by a lady named Sylvie. At about 9p.m., Ronnie and Reggie and a few of their henchmen walked into the club. They looked over at us and nodded and called Sylvie over to the end of the bar where they stood.

They stood speaking to each other for a while before the twins left after having a drink. Sylvie returned to our company white faced and shaken. We asked her what had happened between herself and the twins. She told us that they had told her that they would return once a week to collect cash for their "protection" services. We all knew what that really meant.

On another occassion, I was having a drink in a club in D'Arbly Mews, Soho one evening with a couple of pals of mine, discussing some business. In the club at the same time was a guy from West London, Harry Burford, who was in our company. Harry recently had some business with the Krays concerning a stolen lorry carrying a high value load of scotch and mohair. They had had a disagreement about the money for the load and subsequently fell out. We later learned that a phone call was made from the club to the Krays, telling them that Harry was in the club.

Roughly an hour later someone in the club told Harry that he was wanted downstairs, so he went down. A few minutes later someone came in and asked us if we knew what was going on downstairs in the club. Inquisitively we went down to investigate. As we got outside we saw the Kray twins and a number of their firm running down D'Arbly Mews and into D'Arbly Street. Harry was on the floor; he had received a severe beating and had been cut down one side of his face and across his backside, a favourite method of punishment at the time, as the stitches would break every time the victim sat down.

A friend of Harry's, who was in the club at the time, came down and told us not to ring the police, and assured us that he would take Harry home. We later learned that Harry had received treatment and had been stitched up by a struck-off doctor.

The Krays later claimed they only hurt their own. Well, I know for a fact they would hurt anyone. If they had looked after their own they probably would not have spent so many years in prison. I liked Scotch Ian. He, too, was one of the firm. He went with Ronnie Kray when the gangland boss killed George Cornell in the Blind Beggars pub. Ian got 20 years for his part in the killing. Scotch Ian went back to Scotland when he was released from prison. I hope he has made something of his life away from the Kray twins' clutches. I used to have a few drinks in the Regency Club with Ian and always found him to be a nice bloke.

When the Krays were finally caught, all they kept doing was blaming other people for the crimes they had committed. Even in their books, they have put good people down, trying to kid people that they were nice guys. People have the right to form their own opinions of the Krays, and I hope that they don't feel sorry for those two evil bastards. Like me they knew what they were doing was wrong, and they, like many others, have had to pay for it.

When the Krays were finally arrested on 8th May 1968, Reggie was in bed with a young girl and Ronnie was found with a young boy. Along with their firm, they were taken into custody. The two members of the Krays' firm I felt most sorry for were Ronnie Bender and Chrissy Lambrianou. They kept their mouths shut and Ronnie Kray and his solicitor promised them that no matter what happened they would speak up for them and get their sentences reduced on appeal. It never happened — the Kray twins only cared about themselves.

And I believe I am right in saying that almost everybody in the East End was terrified of them, including me. When the twins later received their 30-year sentences from Mr Justice Melford Stevenson, the old East End came alive again. Hardly anyone here felt sorry for them. Because no matter what their so-called fans say about them today, we in the East End knew what they were really like. We were the ones who had to suffer at their hands.

14

the branding
by ronnie kray

AT THAT TIME I was living in Lea Bridge Road, Hackney. I rented the top half of a house and a mate of mine, Andrew Paul, was staying with me because he had left his wife. He was Italian and he was working as a minder at the Krays' West End club, Esmerelda's Barn. The club in Wilton Place, Knightsbridge, had a lovely bar and there were gambling tables where the rich could play.

But I first met Andy when he was working at the more humble Regency Club in the East End. I usually did jobs by myself, but occasionally I teamed up with a mate of mine. One day me and my mate had a nice little earner.

I went to Harry Abrahams' house but no one answered the door so I went off to the Regency Club in Hackney to see if he or any of the firm were there. I walked into the club and as I went downstairs I saw a member of the Kray gang, Fat Pat, standing at the bar. He was chatting to a young couple. I said hello and Pat got me a drink.

Some fellows were standing at the other end of the bar and they sent us over a drink. Everything seemed fine. It was turning out to be a good night on the town.

I ordered the young man a drink and I turned to the young lady and said, "What would you like to drink, love?" The young man's response was as quick as it was extraordinary — he pulled out a razor and tried to cut me. Pat caught his wrist as he lunged at me.

"Leave it out," I shouted.

He told the young man to leave me alone. He seemed to respond well by putting the blade back in his pocket and we carried on drinking as though nothing had happened. After about half an hour, the young man, whose name was Bonner, asked me if we could have a word in private.

I felt a bit sorry for him so I said OK, but as I led the way to the toilet someone shouted, "Watch your back."

And as I turned, Bonner was just about to cut me down the back with his razor. I dived at the toilet door and luckily for me it went inwards. I fell to the floor, but Bonner was coming at me with the razor still in his hand. As I got to my feet I threw a punch catching him smack in the middle of his nose.

There was blood everywhere.

Just then the club minder came in to see what the fuss was all about. Pat told him what had happened and the minder moved to me and said, "Look, Len, get out of here. There will be murders over all this."

"I haven't done anything. He was going to cut me with a razor," I replied.

He said, "I know, I know you are not to blame, that's why I want you to get out of here. I don't want you to get hurt."

I said OK, and said goodbye to Pat. Then I left pretty sharpish.

I went home and went to bed thinking the whole incident would blow over and soon be forgotten.

At about one o'clock in the morning I was woken up by Andy Paul who had just come home after working a shift at the Krays' club, Esmerelda's Barn in the West End. He came into my room. "Len, you got to get up," he ordered.

"Andy, what are you waking me up for?"

"I have just left Ronnie Kray and he wants you to phone him up.

"Andy, do you know what the time is? What does he want?"

"I don't know. You know they never tell us anything," replied Andy.

I said I would wait until the morning, then go round to Vallance Road, where the twins still lived with their mother, Violet.

Andy added, "Len, you know what Ronnie is like. If you don't do what he tells you there's no telling what he will do." I didn't want to get Andy into trouble so I got up and got dressed and went up the road to a phone box. I called the club and asked for Ronnie. He came on the phone quickly.

"What do you want, Ron?" I asked.

"Get a cab, I want to see you right away and I will pay for the cab."

"Won't it wait until the morning?"

"No. Don't worry, everything is all right."

"OK, I'll get a cab straight away," I replied.

I've regretted those words all my life. Harry Abrahams had always warned me: "Never, ever, ever go and see the twins on your own." Unfortunately I ignored those words of wisdom. I arrived at Esmerelda's Barn at about two o'clock in the morning.

I asked the cab driver to wait, as I didn't think I would be long. I walked into the club. The bar was shut and men were standing on both sides of the wall without drinks in their hands. The gambling tables were closed and as I got half way through the club I sensed that something was wrong. I couldn't turn back. It was too late. "Through there, Len," gestured one of the men.

I went through the doorway and found myself in the kitchen. Ronnie was standing opposite me, surrounded by about a dozen men. I knew a couple of them to be decent blokes, but the rest were yes men, real creeps.

"Come over here, Len, and sit down," ordered Ronnie. So I sat in an old armchair and waited to find out what all the fuss was about.

Ronnie mumbled something about hurting a pal of theirs. I said, "I don't know what you're talking about."

Right then his face changed and he told two big blokes to

117

hold me. Then he moved. He turned around, and I saw that he was standing in front of a gas range cooker and I could see pokers on the gas, which were white hot.

He picked one up and came towards me.

He said, "You've upset me, now you must pay for it."

Without warning Ronnie stabbed my body with the poker.

The heat burnt through my jacket and shirt. I felt a sharp pain across my stomach. I was panic-stricken. He started to burn my hair off and then my suit. He paused, then gripped the poker tight and stabbed me in the left cheek. The pain was immense and unbearable. I could feel the flesh on my cheeks and around my eye melt. My eyebrow was burnt away, the smell was awful. The pain was excruciating. For a moment I thought he was going to stop, but then he put the poker back on the same cheek. Then Ronnie went back to the cooker and picked up the other poker. Now I realised they were cold steels that you sharpened knives on.

I tried to open my eyes, but only the right one opened. He still had that evil smile. I was praying to God for help as I thought, Now he is going to fucking kill me. The heat was tremendous and I could hardly see. His face had an expression on it that I will never forget, not until the day that I die. His eyes were glaring at me and then he roared, "Now, I'm going to burn your fucking eyes out."

I was too shocked and scared to utter a word. But thank God someone did it for me.

"No, Ron, not that!" Someone pleaded from the crowd of henchmen. This seemed to change Ron's mind. I never did find out who saved my life. Ron calmly walked away, and as he did he said, "OK, you can go now." The job was done — I left.

At first I did not realise what he had said, too stunned to take anything in. One of the blokes helped me to my feet and directed me through the doorway. He helped me to the stairs, because the blood was running into my eyes and I could hardly see. I got to the bottom of the stairs and walked out into the main street. The Kray henchman let go of me. I opened my eyes as far as I could. The cabbie was still waiting for me. The cabbie took one look at me and said, "Look, mate, I have a wife and kids. I don't want to get mixed up with this."

I didn't have the strength to reply, but he must have felt sorry for me because he put me in his cab.

We had only gone a short way when the cabbie noticed a car was following us. "Don't worry," I said. "They only want to see where we're going."

They were obviously worried I might go straight to the police.

I told him not to take me home, but to go to Stepney which was where Harry Abrahams and his wife, Jean, lived. I knocked on the door and Jean opened it. As soon as she saw the state I was in she took me into her living room and told me to lie down on the settee. She told me Harry would go mad when he saw what had happened to me.

By now my left eye was closed and my right one was nearly the same. I had big blisters coming up on my face and body.

Jean got some yellow cream for burns and smeared it all over my face. Then she gave me some pain-killing tablets.

When she had finished she looked at me and said, "You don't have to say anything. There's only one person that would do that to anybody."

I heard what she said. I couldn't open my eyes at all now. But I never told her or Harry who assaulted me.

Jean was a marvel. She has now passed away and wherever she is, I want her to know I will never forget what she did for me. God bless her!

Harry came home later on that morning and Jean told him what she thought had happened. He said that he would go immediately to Vallance Road to find out why I had been attacked.

Harry was true to his word, and the next day he went and saw the Kray twins.

I don't know what explanation they gave him for the attack on me.

When Harry came back, he said that Ronnie had said he was sorry and added that when I was better I could go to their club, The Kentucky, in the Mile End Road and have a drink with them. They must have been pleased that I hadn't gone to the Old Bill.

I stayed at Harry's for a couple of weeks. Him and Jean were very good to me. Jean was just like a nurse. The swelling had gone down and the blisters were scabs. My eyes had opened up, but I still had pain in my left eye.

I left Harry's house and went back to my flat in North

London. As I was leaving Jean said to me, "If you get any more pain in that eye, you had better go to Moorfields Eye Hospital. You never know what long term damage there could be."

I said I would and I thanked her for all she had done for me, and off I went.

Some of my mates came round to see me and gave me some money to help me out. They were good thieves, not villains, and they hated the Krays.

Andy Paul came round. He was now back with his wife. He apologised for what had happened. He said he didn't know that Ronnie had planned to torture me. I believed him. Andy said Ronnie was a raving lunatic. And I believed that 'n' all.

Then he told me why I had been targeted for the vicious assault. Apparently the bloke I had the trouble with in the Regency Club was the son of a friend of the Kray twins. His name was Bonner Ward and his father was Buller Ward, another well-known villain in London. After the nightclub clash, Buller Ward and his cronies had come looking for me with guns. Not finding me they had got word to the Krays, and Ron then decided to take the lead in dishing out the punishment.

Sometime later Reggie had a fall out with Buller Ward and cut him about the face in the Regency Club, giving Buller the nickname 'tramlines'.

My left eye was getting worse and I could stand the pain no more, so I went to Moorfields Eye Hospital in Old Street. When I saw the doctor he asked me what had happened. I gave him some cock-and-bull story. I know he didn't believe a word I was saying, but he examined me all the same. The doctor gave me an X-ray and treated my eye and face. He gave me some pain-killing tablets and a patch to wear over my eye. He said I was very lucky not to have lost the eye altogether.

I went back to the hospital for my treatments and had my eye 'popped out' a couple of times during the treatment.

I was a patient at Moorfields Eye Hospital for the next five years and was constantly in pain — a permanent reminder of Ronnie Kray's ferocious temper.

15

albert donoghue

AS FAR AS I knew, Albert Donoghue had always hated the Krays. Everyone thought he was a loyal member of Harry Abrahams' firm. Yet when Harry got his five-year sentence for a bank job, Albert amazed everyone by jumping ship and throwing in his lot with the twins.

This seemed even more unbelievable because Reggie Kray had shot Albert, supposedly over the attack on me. Albert has written in his autobiography that Reggie shot him in the foot because he and Harry Abrahams went round to the Krays' house armed with guns. I truly believe that was a lie because I know that Harry never ever carried a gun.

Another gripe of mine with Albert's autobiography is when he wrote about the time when he was on the Krays' firm and he came to see me to ask me for some money for 'one of the chaps' who had come out of prison. I was supposed to have given him a fiver, and he was supposed to have taken another twenty quid off me. Well that's another lie. In those days, if someone came out of prison and you were holding money, no one would have to ask you for money, you would automatically slip whoever it was a few quid. He also said that every time the twins hurt someone, that person would end up on the Krays' firm and that wasn't true either.

He even claimed that I joined the Krays' firm. So, to set the record straight, I was never on the Krays' firm. I admit I was a thief but I didn't go about shooting people or cutting them up.

About six weeks after the branding attack I was getting fed up of sitting indoors, so I got myself dressed up and went to the Regency to have a drink. I thought, I'm not going to hide for the rest of my life.

It was early when I walked in and there weren't a lot of people inside. I went to the bar and ordered a drink. Mickey Barry was behind the bar serving and he gave me a large vodka and orange and slipped me a few quid.

He was a nice chap, one of the four brothers who owned the club. In fact, all the Barrys were nice chaps. Johnny Barry had been a fish porter at Billingsgate Fish Market when I had worked down there.

While I was at the bar, Lenny the Singing Waiter came in. He used to collect the empty glasses and bring your drinks to the table. Everybody liked him. The club was beginning to fill up now and the band started playing. When the resident singer saw me, he sung my favourite song, 'When My Little Girl is Smiling' as he always did when I was there.

A few people came over and spoke to me. Some said what a liberty Ronnie had taken, others were too frightened to say anything as the Krays had their spies in the club, who would report straight back to them.

The barmaid gave me a drink. "It's from that chap over there," she said.

He came over and it was Bonner Ward. He said he was sorry for what Ronnie had done supposedly in revenge for the fight with me. We had a couple of drinks together and made our peace. Shame we hadn't made it six weeks earlier! A few months later a mate of mine came round to see me. He said he was skint and did I know anyway that he could get a few bob.

I felt sorry for him so I told him I had a job lined up and he could come with me. A couple of weeks later we did the job and got a few grand each.

So I was doing the odd job, and after the branding, the Krays once sent two fellows to see me, to see if they could get a few quid off me when they heard that I had had a good 'tickle'. However, I obviously wanted to keep my distance from the Krays.

There was a turn-up for the books, though, as, shortly after Ron's attack, his twin, Reggie Kray, paid me a visit and offered me a hundred quid. He put the money in my top pocket. I refused to accept the cash, but Reggie said, "I thought we were mates."

"I have done nothing against you," I replied.

And then Reg had the audacity to ask, "If you ever hear anyone slag us off, will you let us know?"

I thought the hundred quid was a bit of an insult. I walked to a nearby pub, banged the roll of cash on the bar and, gesturing towards a few senior citizens seated there, said to the barman, "Buy these old people as many drinks as they want."

16

other members of the kray firm

DESPITE RONNIE'S vicious attack on me, I was still on friendly terms with a couple of men on the Krays' firm who had not been present on the night of the branding.

One was Connie Whitehead, who was with them for a long time. He was a nice bloke, with fair hair, good looking and a nice build. In later years he had a gambling club in Aldgate.

One night I decided to have a gamble there and my luck was in — I won all the money. I skinted all the others punters and took my money from the club that night. Connie came over to me and said, "Well Len, you have cleaned us all out. I have never seen anything like that happen in any spiel."

He shook my hand and wished me good luck. Connie was Ronnie Kray's driver for a while during the heyday of the twins.

Once I met him and a couple of his mates when I walked into the little pub in Sutton Street in Stepney. They were having a good old laugh. They got me a drink and I enjoyed their company.

We'd already put away quite a few drinks when the phone behind the bar rang. The guv'nor of the pub called Connie to tell him he was wanted on the phone. When Connie came back he said he had to go as Ronnie Kray needed a driver. Connie looked frustrated.

I felt sorry for Connie as I knew he wanted to get away from the Krays, but he realised he couldn't break free — they don't let go that easily. Once you had committed yourself then that was it; you only left the firm when the Krays had no more use for you.

I always liked Connie and so did a lot of people in the East End. He later did eight years for being with the Krays. He has since moved away from the East End and is now a very hard-working businessman and people have a lot of respect for him. He once owned the Astor Club in Canning Town. I am happy for him because he, like other members of the firm, did a lot of bird for the Kray twins, and never got a penny from them for all the trouble.

Fat Pat was another firm member who I had a lot of time for. He was big, fat, loveable man and had a nice way about him. Pat was always kind to me and it made me wonder why some of these blokes were on the firm, because they weren't all bad.

Little Nobby Clark was with the Krays for a long time. He

was like one of the family and I know that he was very loyal to the Krays. He was an ex-boxer and very well respected in the East End. Everybody liked him, but like so many others, the Krays turned on him and finished up shooting him in the foot. The trouble with the Krays was they didn't trust anybody, not even their friends.

17

george
cornell

I HAD ARRANGED to meet two blokes in a little drinking club adjacent to Billingsgate Fish Market. They had to give me some money for some gear they had taken off me. It was a nice little club, owned by a Jewish woman.

When I went in, the men were standing at the bar. I told them that I had come for the money they owed me. They were a tasty pair who could have a fight if needs be. They had already had a few drinks and were trying to give me less money than we had agreed. I was having none of it, so I said, "I want me money or me gear back."

I wasn't very confident they were going to agree. But what could I do?

Just then the door opened and of all people who walked in but George Cornell. He cut an imposing figure with his

Frank Sinatra hat on. If there was one man I wanted to see at that time, it was him. I went over to have a chat with George, bought him a drink and said I would catch up on old times when I had finished my business.

When I got back to the two blokes one of them said, "Hey, that's George Cornell. Do you know him that well?"

I replied that I did. Their attitude changed immediately. They got a round of drinks in, paid me the money in full and left pretty sharpish. George was a very hard man and people were wary of him. I went over to George and told him what had happened. He burst out laughing and said, "At least you got your money."

From that day on, every time I saw the two men in the pub they would get me a drink and we became good friends.

I liked George Cornell and I also liked Jack 'The Hat' McVitie. Both met grisly ends at the hands of the Kray twins. Neither George or Jack ever did me a bad turn and I always say, speak as you find. I had felt that way about the Krays until Ronnie tortured me with the red hot pokers.

18

jack `the hat´ mcvitie

MILLIE ANSWERED THE phone. A voice said, "Who's that?" I knew it was Jack, he was never one to stand on ceremony. I told him that I had just got home. He said he had got hold of a few quid and was going to Dartmoor Prison the next day to pay a visit to a mate of his. He asked me if I wanted to go for the ride.

I told him to hang on a minute, and put my hand over the receiver. I told Millie what Jack had said. She told me that if I went with Jack I could visit her son Harry while we were there and that I could borrow her car. I told Jack this and he said, "Lovely, I'll be over to you at four o'clock in the morning."

Millie knocked on my door at 3 a.m. the next morning with a nice pot of tea. I had a bath, got dressed and was ready to go. Jack arrived right on time and off we went.

We stopped on the way to Dartmoor Prison and bought some bottles of drink, some cigarettes, tobacco and food — what prisoners call a joey.

We made up a nice parcel and a few pounds inside for both men. When we got to the prison we were shown into a little shed where we had to wait to be called. Our names came up and off we went. The visit went well and we gave the prisoner their joeys.

We stopped off in Yeovil on the way back to London. Jack wanted a drink. We found a very attractive hotel-cum-pub and had a nice meal with a few drinks. Jack had got the flavour so we had a few more drinks. We got chatting with the manager and he asked us where we were from.

Jack said we'd been to Her Majesty's prison in Dartmoor and before he could say anything else I butted in. "Yes, we've been up there to look for some locations for a film that we are thinking of making."

The manager asked what the film was going to be called. "'The One that Got Away,'" Jack replied, quick as a flash. We kept a straight face, and after a short while we went to the toilet. We burst out laughing as soon as the door was shut.

When we went back to the bar, the manager was pouring us a drink. It was getting late and as we had had quite a lot to drink we booked a room with two single beds for the night. I phoned Millie and told her what had happened. She was pleased everything had gone well. The hotel manager showed us our room — it was really grand. We said goodnight and went to bed.

Arriving home the next day I dropped Jack off at a pub in North London and went home. I thanked Millie for the loan of her car and told her that the visit with her son Harry had gone off OK, and we had dropped him off a joey.

Jack 'The Hat' was by now really beginning to annoy the Kray twins. Their spies were reporting back to them that he was constantly mouthing off about them. The last straw seems to have come when he ripped the twins off whilst carrying out a job for them. They couldn't afford to lose face like this; something had to be done otherwise everyone would start to take liberties, and their empire built on fear would crumble like a house of cards.

I had seen at first hand how much Jack disliked the Kray twins. He didn't like being bossed around by men much younger than he was. No one thought he would ever threaten them to their face, but I saw how his anger was for real and how he did intend to cause them harm.

I once bought a gun for Jack. I was at a party in the East End when word came to me that a chap had a gun to sell. It was a service revolver and I bought it from him intending to give it to Jack because I knew he liked guns.

I was living in East Ham at the time and got word to Jack to come and see me. Within a couple of days, Jack was knocking at the door. I let him in and gave him his present. He loved it. But then it was his turn to surprise me.

"I want to show you something," he said conspiratorially.

He went outside to his car and came back and showed me his surprise — a hand grenade.

His face beamed with delight. "Len, see this? I've only got to pull the pin and boom — they're dead meat!"

It didn't take a genius to figure out who 'they' were.

He told me he was going to lie in wait for the Kray twins one night and blow them to hell. I told him that he couldn't do that as he could easily hurt innocent people.

I think he was serious about attempting to kill the Krays with the hand grenade so perhaps I saved their lives, as well as preventing the slaughter of innocent people who might have been nearby.

Jack accepted my reasoning but added, "I will have to think of another way to dispose of them. If they were taken out that would be the end of the Kray twins' firm. A lot of people's worries would be over."

I am not sure if Jack was really intent on killing the Kray twins, but of course, the Krays got Jack first.

Jack had annoyed the Krays for years. For instance, he was once sent with George Osbourne to shoot Leslie Payne, who the twins thought was going to grass on them.

Jack and George went to Payne's house and knocked on the door. Payne was out and his wife opened the door. Jack and George left it at that. But Jack make the mistake of keeping the money the Krays had given him and then went about telling everyone who would listen how he had turned over the Krays and kept the cash. Obviously the twins weren't too impressed with Jack.

Unbeknown to some of their firm, the Kray twins had already decided Jack's fate that fateful night. Now the Krays' plan was set in motion. Ronnie Bender was told by Ronnie Kray to meet them at the Cheshire Arms pub. This he did, because one thing you never did was let the twins down or you would suffer the consequences.

Bender arrived at the pub between 10.30 and 11 p.m. On entering the pub, he was greeted by Ronnie Kray and given a drink and told that they were all going round to Blonde Carol's house for a party. Bender was unaware that this night would change his life forever, and for the worse. The Lambrianou brothers, Tony and Chrissy, were given orders by the Krays to go to the Regency Club, which was just around the corner from Blonde Carol's house in Evering Road, Stoke Newington. They were to wait there until Jack the Hat turned up. When he did, they were to tell him that they were going to a party at Blonde Carol's house.

Knowing Jack as they did, they knew that he loved a party and would not refuse. The Krays' plan was now swinging into action. It was getting late and after they had finished their drinks and the Krays had popped their pills, the firm was on the move. First to arrive at the house were the Krays, their cousin Ronnie Hart, Ronnie Bender and the two Mills brothers. Blonde Carol was sent over the road to her friend's house and was told not to return until the next day. They simply commandeered her house giving her orders to vacate her own home. That just goes to show you how much fear the Kray twins could put into people. Word was sent round to the Regency Club to tell the Lambrianou brothers that the party was in full swing. When Jack the Hat finally arrived at the Regency, he had already had a few drinks, and when he was told by the Lambrianous that there was a party going on at Carol's, he was all for it, because Jack did love a party.

The Kray twins were now in position and poor old Jack was on his way to a party that never was. Little did he know that once inside that house, the only way he would be coming out would be feet first and dead. Jack's car had pulled up round the corner from Blonde Carol's house. Out he got with the Lambrianou brothers as his escort. Ronnie Hart was upstairs as a lookout, and when they arrived he ran downstairs and told the Kray twins that they were coming. Jack went down the stairs to the basement with Chrissy and Tony Lambrianou behind him. On entering the house he was shown where to go. With that, he pushed the door open and in he went, not knowing what was in store for him. "Right," Jack shouted, "where are the booze and the birds?" But there were no booze or birds, just the Krays with some of their firm. By now Jack had realised what was going on. He was grabbed by two of the firm and was pulled back across the room, where the Krays had him pinned up against the wall. Reggie Kray, with a gun in his hand, put it against Jack's head and pulled the trigger, but to the twins' amazement, the gun didn't go off. A scuffle broke out and Jack's elbow went through the window smashing it.

By now the twins had lost complete control of themselves. There was Reggie screaming at Jack the Hat to be a man, and poor Jack screaming back, "I am a man, but I don't want to die like one." There was Ronnie Kray shouting, "Go on, Reg, kill the fucking bastard." At that moment someone put a large knife in Reggie's hand. Jack had no chance against the Krays on his own. Reggie plunged the knife into Jack's face again and again. The blood was pouring down Jack's face, one of his eyes was hanging out, and still Ronnie Kray was screaming, "Go on, Reg, kill the bastard. I've done my one, now do yours."

Without any hesitation Reggie plunged the knife again and again into Jack's body and Ronnie was still screaming like the lunatic he was. By now Jack's body was going limp because of all the blood he had lost, and as his body was slowly dropping to the floor, Reggie Kray thrust the knife into Jack's body ripping half his stomach out. As Jack's body finally fell to the floor, Reggie Kray bent over his body and with one last thrust in anger, he slashed Jack's throat from ear to ear. Jack's lifeless body lay there in a pool of blood. Now that their evil premeditated crime was over, the Kray twins began giving out their orders. They told Ronnie Bender to get rid of the body and all the evidence of that night's murder. They had the bloody cheek to tell him to carry the blood-soaked body out of the house, carry it three to four hundred yards down the road, and dump it over the railway line, in the hope that when a train came along, it would mangle the body enough that the police would not be able to make out the real cause of death. Albert Donaghue was told to strip off the wallpaper and redecorate the room. I think at that time they were all in such a state of shock that they just did as they were told. They knew, quite rightly, that the Krays could just as easily have turned on them. What a pair of callous bastards they really were, not even having the guts to clean up their own dirty work.

After giving their orders, they fled the scene and left Ronnie Bender and Chrissy Lambrianou there on their own, Ronnie Bender not knowing what to do and Chrissy sitting on the stairs crying. I do honestly believe that some of the firm that were present at that horrible crime really thought that the Krays were only going to give Jack the Hat a severe talking to and a beating. While Bender and Chrissy were standing there looking down onto Jack's blood-soaked body, Tony Lambrianou came back to the scene and the trio then set about their task. Chrissy went upstairs and took the eiderdown off the bed and wrapped Jack's body in it. They then wrapped the body in the blood-stained carpet. As they got out into the street, a black man walked by unaware of the evil that had taken place that night.

They eventually got Jack's body into the back of his own car. Chrissy said to Ronnie Bender, "You drive the car and we will follow you in ours." Ronnie Bender was having none of that, so Tony Larnbrianou decided that he would drive the car with Jack's body in it. Because they had to get away from the murder scene, they decided to dump it somewhere over south London; one more body would not stand out so much with all the shootings going on over there. They drove the car through the East End and under the River Thames through the Rotherhithe Tunnel, dumping the car with Jack's body inside it outside a church.

All sorts of stories were put about in the East End to explain Jack's disappearance. One tale was that Jack had run away with another woman, another was that he had mishandled some gelignite in his car and blown himself to kingdom come. Little did they know that poor old Jack 'The Hat' McVitie was dead, another victim of the Kray twins.

Every time they hurt someone really badly, the Krays would have a story put about that the chap they had hurt was no good. In Jack's case they had it put about that he was only a tuppenny-ha'penny crook.

Well I knew different. He was a good money-getter. He didn't deserve to die in that horrific way. I know Jack took a few liberties in his time, but he was no different to a lot of others in those days. I could name a lot of people who did the same.

By now people were calling the Krays the untouchables and it looked as if they could get away with anything — even murder.

The story was that they had enough bent Old Bill on

their side to help them if they got into trouble with the law. But they forgot one thing — you can only push people so far and then something gives.

19

a word in
my ear
from the
old bill

ONE NIGHT I went to the Regency Club for a drink and met Jack the Hat. All his friends knew that he had gained the nickname because he always wore a hat to cover his bald patch. He used to have a lovely mop of hair. We had a few drinks and I told him I was going down to the south coast for a couple of weeks.

"I've already hired a car so if you're not doing anything special, come with me," I suggested to him. He quickly agreed.

We went home, put some clothes in a case and off we went. We drove down to Dover and stayed there for the night, had a nice drink in the hotel bar, then went to bed. We had our breakfast in the morning, paid our bill and left.

Next stop was Brighton. We booked into a four-star hotel and toured the drinking clubs. We stayed there for three days and then we were off again. We arrived in Bournemouth late in the afternoon. Jack said he had to make a phone call so we pulled up at a phone kiosk.

When he came out he said, "Sorry, Len, I've got to go home." He said he had a job lined up that he didn't want to miss.

I drove him to the railway station and made sure he had some money.

I stayed with him until his train came in. We said our goodbyes and I went back to Bournemouth and booked into a nice hotel.

I had been there a couple of days and was having a drink at the hotel bar, when the bartender informed me there was a good club nearby called The Candlelight. So I got a cab and went there. It was a swanky club, done up really well.

I was shown to a table and ordered some drinks. There was a party going on at the tables near me and, as I was on my own, they asked me to join them. We were all having a lovely time, but as it was getting late. I asked the waiter to call me a cab.

While I was staying goodbye, the governor of the club asked me where I was staying. I told him. He said a friend of his owned a country club and if I wanted to stay there he would arrange it. Next morning I checked out of my hotel and we all went to this country club. It was about a mile's drive through the grounds before you got there, and then right in front of me was this big mansion. It was called Ossley Manor. I stayed there for a week.

On the Sunday night I told them I would be leaving first thing Monday morning and asked them to give me an early call at 5 a.m. as I wanted to miss the traffic. I set off at about 5.30 in the morning, but driving through the grounds, I came upon a big clearing. The police were everywhere.

I was told to get out of the car. As I did, they handcuffed me, put me in a police car and took me to Lyndhurst nick. No one told me what on earth was going on.

I was put in a cell. Then in came the heavy mob. They put me into a room and told me to sit at the table.

"Right, we nicked a couple of your pals the other day with ninety grand in the boot of their car," one said.

I didn't have a clue what he was talking about.

"You have been staying at the Manor and you've been spending quite a lot of money," one of the cops said, as if I didn't know.

"So what, it's my money. I can do what I like, it's a free country."

Silence enveloped the room until one of the officers said;

"We are not going to get anything out of him. Take him back to the cells."

A little while later the cell door was opened and they took me back into the interrogation room. Now they were being very nice to me, asking me if I would like a cup of tea.

I said, "Yes please." And they put a packet of fags on the table.

"Now, Len, let's get this all cleared up," said the officer

"OK," I said, ever anxious to help.

"Is that your car you've been driving around in these past weeks?"

"You know it's not. You must have searched it and found the hire agreement papers in there."

"All right, what is your home address in London?"

So I told them. They asked me what was I doing down there, so I told them I was on a two-week holiday.

Then came the big question. "Where are you getting all this money from that you're spending?"

"Out of the bank," I replied. By now I was getting fed up.

"I've told you what you want to know, now you tell me what I am doing here," I shouted.

"We have reason to believe you are one of the Great Train Robbers."

"You must be joking!" I spluttered in utter astonishment. After a few minutes silence, they took me back to the cells. I had been there for two or three hours when they came back for me again.

"You didn't tell us you had done bird."

"You never asked me," I replied.

They told me they had checked my address and found I had been telling them the truth. They had checked the bank and found out I had again been telling the truth about the money that I had been spending so freely on the south coast.

They gave me back my property and told me I was free to go.

I turned to the officer in charge. "Before I go, can you tell me what made you think I was a train robber?"

He said someone at the Manor had phoned them up and was after a reward.

"Well, now you can phone them back and tell them that this is not their lucky day. Goodbye."

And out I walked.

I had left my flat in north London and taken a room in a house off Bow Road in Addiscombe Road, with a woman I knew who used to put up long-distance lorry drivers. Her name was Millie. She was a lovely woman, 'one of your own' as we say in the East End. Her son Harry was doing time in Dartmoor.

I got back to London and went straight home. Millie, my landlady, was just making a cup of tea.

"Hi there!" I said. "I hope you've got one there for me. How are you?"

I explained what had happened during my trip down south. Then she told me that during my absence, loads of police had come to her house, searched my room and asked a few questions.

"All the neighbours were out in the street — it was a right carnival," she said.

I went to the off-licence for some drink and we had a good old laugh over it all.

I saw Jack the Hat later and told him what had happened.

"I'm glad I came back when I did," he said.

I asked him how things had gone on his job.

"OK, we all got a nice few quid."

He offered me some money, but I told him I still had a bundle stashed away. The following week I went to see Hubby Davis and got my old driving job back. I thought this would keep the Old Bill off my back. I was only there a couple of days though.

I was driving to Purfleet Rolling Mills bringing back reels of paper for the newspapers in Fleet Street, and on the third day, as I pulled into the yard, Patsy, the yard foreman, came running over to me. "Len, get out of the lorry," he shouted. "You're wanted in the office right away."

As I walked to the office I saw a big Humber car parked outside. This was no ordinary visit from the Old Bill. I knew it was the Flying Squad. All sorts of things went through my mind.

My first thought was that they had come to question me about a job I had done a few weeks ago. "Well, here goes," I said to myself.

I went into the office and was shown immediately into the governor's office. Inside were the four Davis brothers and these two big guys. You could tell instantly they were police.

"Come in, Len, and sit here," said Hubby Davis.

Then one of the big guys introduced himself.

"My name is Alf Durrell and I'm from the Flying Squad."

"I'm Lenny Hamilton from Bow," I replied with a smile on my face, trying to disguise my nervousness.

Well, you should have seen their faces — they had to laugh.

Then Hubby said, "Two gangsters came here this afternoon

asking if you worked here. I told them to mind their own business. One of them said he would chop off my ears and they said you owed the Krays two grand and they wanted the money."

It was news to me that I owed the Krays any money.

Hubby said he had telephoned the police immediately after the visit of the imposing pair, one of whom I later discovered to be Johnny Squibb, an associate of the Krays.

The officer then asked me what was going on.

Alf Durrell stepped in. "I have been looking everywhere for you. You were the one that Ronnie Kray burnt with the pokers."

"That's in the past," I told him.

"What is it, Lenny? Have you had a nice little tickle recently? They must have heard about it."

"You must be joking," was my reply. "That's why I am working here. I need the money."

He told me he badly wanted to bring the Krays to justice and that I could help him to nail at least one of them. He went on about what a terrible thing Ronnie had done to me and how people were saying what a liberty it was.

He asked me if I would make a statement against Ronnie.

"You must be joking," I said.

He remained silent and seeing I wouldn't change my mind he let me walk out of the office.

Bow Road nick was on the corner of our street and as I walked along I saw a car I knew belonged to the twins.

I got to my door and let myself in. Millie called me into her

private room. "Len, a big fat chap came here asking for you."
I knew she was describing Fat Pat who worked for the twins.

She had told him to fuck off. That was our Millie.

I got up the next morning and climbed over the back
gardens, dropping into Bow Road, and I caught the tube to
Wapping. When I went into the yard, Patsy Davis said,
"Hello Len. Sorry but you're not out today. Hubby wants to
see you."

At about one o'clock I was in the yard helping to load and
unload some trailers when I was told to report to the office.
Hubby and Solly Davis were there and so were the two
policemen from the Flying Squad. This was becoming a
habit.

Alf Durrell said, "We have kept watch on your address and
we noticed a car hanging about. We know and we know you
know who they are. Don't you?"

"Yes," I mumbled. "They know I am on my own and that's
why they can get away with it."

"Well, do something about it to protect yourself," said
Durrell.

I asked how.

Durrell explained. "You make a statement and sign it. I will
go to the Kentucky Club and I will show it to the twins and
tell them that if a hair on your head is touched this will be
brought out against them. I will tell them to get their cronies
to lay off you."

I pondered for a moment. "If you try to use that in court I
will say I had to sign it under duress."

Durrell swore to me that he would not use the statement in any other way.

I added, "If I do it, people will say I'm a grass."

"Don't be silly. A lot of people are on your side, and the worst thing the Krays can do is to hurt you again. In fact, they will make it their business to see that no harm comes to you."

"What the hell," I thought and I made the statement and signed it. The police read it back to me, then Durrell put it in his pocket.

I kept asking myself, Have I done the right thing?

I was kept in the yard that day and at about five o'clock in came the big Humber car. I saw the police get out and they were laughing as they went into the office. Half an hour later I was called in; they were having a drink. They gave me one and boy did I need it.

Then we all sat down and Durrell told me he had been to see the twins. He had shown them a copy of the statement and told Ronnie, "You had better look after that boy because if he so much as gets even a push, I will be breathing down your fucking necks. You ought to have seen their faces as I walked out."

Durrell added, "Reggie is coming to see you tonight at seven o'clock. Don't worry, me and my mate will be there. I will come and knock for you when he arrives."

He dropped me home in their car. When I got in I told Millie what had happened and that I had signed a statement. "Good luck to you," she said.

I said I would move out if she wanted me to, but she told me I could stay as long as I liked.

Later, I was in my room getting dressed when Millie knocked on the door and said, "Len, there is a police officer at the door asking for you."

It was dead on seven o'clock when everyone arrived. Durrel said, "Reggie and Charlie are outside. Don't worry, we are there with you."

I shut the front door and went with him. As promised the Kray brothers were there, in their big green Mercedes car. As soon as they saw me, they both got out. Reggie, straight to the point, said to me, "What is the matter? What did you have to go and do that for? Ain't we all friends?"

"Look, Reg," I replied. "What Ronnie did to me, I think I took it well. I never went to the police even though a lot of people wanted me to, even some of your own firm, but I stood by the code. You don't grass! Now two of your firm have come to my workplace, I know who they are. What am I supposed to do?"

Reggie said, "You can come and have a drink in the club anytime and let people see that we are friends." With that he put a hundred quid in my top pocket. He and Charlie, who had remained silent, got in their car and left. Alf Durrell walked towards me, and I told him what Reggie had said.

Durrell put his hands on my shoulder and said, "You haven't got a worry in the world. It's more than they dare do, to touch you now."

And as he was walking away, he added, "Don't worry, I

have told them I will come and see you to make sure everything is all right."

I went to the Green Dragon gambling club in Whitechapel. A couple of rummy games were going on, and Billy Ackerman was there. He called me to one side and asked me what was going on.

I told him to mind his own business and I walked out. He was one I would never trust. I called him an 'arsehole crawler'.

I packed the job in at Davis Brothers, I gave Millie a couple of months rent and went to Jersey for a couple of weeks. It was nice to get away from it all.

Sitting on the beach at St Owens, I thought how peaceful it was here, like being in heaven, well away from the Krays and all the hassle that had been enveloping my life for the past few years.

When I got back to England my troubles hit me straightaway. Millie told me that a tall man had come to see me the previous week and had left a phone number for me to contact him. Millie made a lovely roast dinner and I went to bed. For the next couple of months I was left alone and the visits from the Krays and the police seemed to have stopped.

But one night, when I was in the White Horse Pub in Burdett Road, I met a bloke called Connie Riley. He was straight and working for a woman who owned a company. They were having an affair.

We had a few drinks and he asked me where I was living.

I said I was getting fed up where I was as it was very noisy with the constant sound of lorries coming and going outside. Connie told me he lived in Forest Gate. The people who owned the house were in show business and they were away most of the time on tour. The only person he saw was the woman who came to clean the house twice a week. Connie said there was a vacant room in the house if I wanted to move in.

He was the only lodger, so if I took the room it would be company for both of us. Connie took me to the house and when I saw the room I fell in love with it. It was spotless and the house was situated in a nice quiet street. I told Millie I might be moving out and living with a mate of mine, and said to her that I would never forget her after all she had done for me. She had looked after me and had been like a mother to me for quite a while.

A week went by and I was doing a bit of running about. I bought myself a car to get about in. Connie had phoned me and left a message to meet in the White Horse pub. I went home, packed my bags, and put them in the car. I said goodbye to Millie — she had tears in her eyes and I promised to come back and see her and to keep in touch.

I got to the flat. Connie helped me in with my bags and helped me to unpack. He never had many clothes so I gave him a couple of suits and a jumper. He was well pleased. His young lady lived in a house in Hornchurch, Essex — with her husband. I used to meet Connie at the White Hart in Hornchurch. It was well out of the way along some country lanes.

The White Hart's governor name was called Reg. He was a nice enough bloke, an ex-tanker driver. I soon made the White Hart my regular pub. Connie and I were in there every night. One day I was having a drink with Reg at the bar and he asked me if I liked to bet.

"Of course I do," I replied. It seemed a bit of a stupid question to me.

He said he had a good tip for a horse the next day and the person who gave it to him had said it couldn't lose. The next morning I got a paper and the horse was priced at 10-8. When I got to the bookies the price was 10 to 1. I took the odds for £500. The horse was in the 2.30 race, so I went to have a drink with Reg. It was nearly three o'clock and Reg phoned his bookie to find out how the horse had got on. He came back with a big smile on his face and I knew the horse had won.

He gave us all a drink. I told him I had £20 to win. "That's good," he said.

If only he had known, I'd just won five grand!

I gave a party in there on Saturday night to celebrate. Reg's wife did all the food and I went down to Billingsgate Fish Market and bought some bowls of jellied eels, prawns, cockles and smoked salmon.

My sister Rose lived in Hornchurch. I hadn't seen her for ages, so I went to see her and told her and her husband to come to the party. She didn't drink and her husband wasn't a drinker either, he just had the odd one, but they both came.

My sister only had orange juice. We all had a good time that night, and it was lovely to see one of my sisters. Reg got an extension for the party and my sister tasted a drop of champagne, but didn't like it.

I went back there on Sunday lunchtime and it was packed. Everybody was saying what a good time they had had and they were all buying me drinks. I settled up with Reg for the party, which didn't cost me as much as I had thought it would. Life was going well, away from the Kray twins and the pressures of the East End.

But I couldn't keep away from the old place. It was getting near Christmas, so I called in at the 81 Club in the Mile End Road to see a few old faces.

Everybody was asking where I'd been, but I never told them.

I made a book in the rummy game, and ended up winning a few hundred pounds

I treated some of the old people in there and we went next door to the Three Crowns for a drink. It was nice to have a jar with some of our old pals, Connie Nunn, Sammy Lewis, Johnny Adshead and a few more.

They were all nice people and you always had a good old laugh with them. They were the true old cockneys of the East End.

This visit went well and I went back to Hornchurch.

Sitting in the White Hart, I told Fred I had been to the East End and won a few quid playing cards. As I was getting a drink, two chaps came in. They knew someone I was with, so

I got them a drink.

During the conversation they mentioned they had some electric guitars to sell, as they needed the money to buy their wives and kids some Christmas presents.

I felt sorry for them so I bought the lot. I thought I could help them and maybe make a few quid for myself as well. But a couple of days later two police officers came in the pub and arrested me for handling stolen property. They took me to Romford nick and I was charged. I went to court. I had to plead guilty and the judge sentenced me to 18 months' imprisonment.

The police said to me that if I told them who I got them from they could speak to the judge and get me a lighter sentence. But I was angry for being duped, and replied, "Go to hell." I was not a grass.

20

pentonville

I ARRIVED at Pentonville nick a week before Christmas. First you have to see the doctor when you go in. You take off your clothes, put a towel around you then drop it when ordered. So there I was, standing there starkers. Then the doctor says bend over, he holds your balls and you cough.

He asks you if you have had any diseases and you say, "No." He says, "OK, A1."

When you are finished with the doctor you go to collect your prison clothes. I was lucky, I knew one of the cons passing out the gear, so he sorted me out some nice clothes and a new pair of shoes.

Then we were taken to our landings.

I was put on B Wing on the fours. When the screw opened

the cell there was a bloke in there. He stunk and there was paper all over the floor.

I put my gear down on the landing. The screw came back.

"I'm not going to sleep in there," I said defiantly.

"If you don't I will put you in the block."

I said, "OK" and with that I was marched to the detention block which was also called the chokey. As least it was clean. I was taken before the Governor in the morning and I told him the cell wasn't fit for a pig to live in.

"Nevertheless you failed to carry out an order," he said giving me seven days in the chokey block and loss of privileges for seven days.

"I haven't had any privileges yet," I protested.

So he gave me another three days on top of the seven for insolence which meant I would be in there over Christmas. I was taken to the chokey block and given my Peter.

One of the screws said to me, "You've started off well." Everyone's a comic.

In your Peter you had a wooden table and chair, bible, plastic mug, plate, a pot to do your bodily functions in and a mattress which was kept outside the cell till eight o'clock at night.

They woke you up at 6 a.m. You slopped out, then had a shave. They brought your breakfast round. Then you were banged up. At seven thirty you slopped out, putting your tray outside your cell. About ten o'clock the doctor came round, putting his head in the cell. "How are you today, no complaints?" and that was it. The door banged shut.

And that's how it went on from day to day.

I finished my ten days in the chokey block and was taken before the Governor. "I hope you've learned your lesson and you can go back on the wing. Have you anything to say?"

I had. "If you put me back in that cell again I will be back in front of you and you will be sending me back down the block."

He then told me I had been re-allocated to a wing that had a single cell. I was well pleased.

I was in my cell putting my gear away when a voice behind me said, "You all right, mate?" When I turned round I was surprised to see Lenny, the singing waiter from the Regency Club. We had a good chat about the old times and I told him what had happened. He gave me some tobacco, papers and matches that you split into four to make them last. That morning I was taken to see the doctor, then I was given my place of work, which was the mailbag shop.

I was taken there that afternoon and given some string and wax, which you pulled the string through to make it easier to pull through the sacking, and a big curved upholsterer's needle.

I was taken to see the screw in charge. He sat on a box high in the air so he could see what was going on all over the shop and told me there was no talking. If I wanted to go to the toilet, I shouldn't shout, just put up my hand.

After three months I was called in front of the Governor. He told me he was putting me on an outside party to work.

"I hope you do not abuse the trust I am giving you."

"No, sir, I won't," I replied.

I had a visit from a mate of mine that week. I was to be going to Epping every day to Hill Hall Women's Open Prison to work, with the outside party. My friend said, "Don't worry, Len, I will find it and bring you some food, tobacco and some drink."

Well, Monday morning came and our cells were opened up to slop out and shave. We had our breakfast and when they had banged up all the other cons I was led down the Centre. It was called the Centre because the screws had an office there. If there was any trouble in the prison, a bell would ring, and they would all run to that spot forming a big circle and no con was allowed to walk across it. You had to walk around it.

We were all lined up, about a dozen of us. The screw who was in charge that week was the one on duty when I was in the chokey block.

When he saw me he said, "Hello, who have we got here then?"

I thought, This is it, he's going to take me off the party.

He took me to one side and asked me, "Can you make a cup of tea?"

"I hope so sir," I replied without looking as insulted as I felt.

"Right, you will be in charge of the food and you had better make a good cup of tea."

Me and three other cons went into the kitchen to pick up our stores. These consisted of two tea urns to make tea in, milk, a bag of tea, a tray of sandwiches, and some rock cakes.

While we were doing this I saw an old mate of mine from the East End.

It was Davey Levy. He gave me a wink and I smiled back. We were taken out of the prison yard and put on a lorry. We loaded the gear onto the back and off we went.

It was nice to be outside again, away from the nick. When we got to Hill Hall, the screw took us to a wooden hut. We unloaded the food and he told me that this was where I would be working, and he gave me the times when the cons would be coming in for their food. He took the others and showed them what they would be doing, saying that he didn't want trouble while we were out there.

If we saw any of the women prisoners, we were not allowed to speak to them. They stayed in a big old mansion on the grounds.

That Friday the screw gave us all the afternoon off. Some played football and some sat in the hut playing cards. When it was time to go, we loaded the gear onto the truck again. The screw called us all together and said he was pleased with the way we had all got stuck in. He said to me, "Son, you really know how to make a good cup of tea." And he told us that we would have a new screw each week. He then gave each of us half an ounce of tobacco that was a perk from the Governor, and we were told we would receive that amount each week.

It was my job to take the empty cans back to the kitchen. When I got there, Davey was in there. He was a nice bloke. He said he was sorry to hear what Ronnie Kray had done to me and related to me about the fight he had had with Reggie. Reggie had stabbed him in the chest in his sister's house in Bow Common Lane.

We went back to our cells, put our working clothes away, and went down to get our dinner. It was pretty good because you got extras for being on an outside party, and the food was cooked better.

It was Saturday and all the outside party were called down to the Governor's office.

We went down one at a time. When it was my turn, he told me that the chief screw, Mr Hutchinson, was pleased with us for the way we worked outside.

He asked me how I liked the job, and I said fine.

"By the way, Hamilton," he said, "you will be leaving your single cell today."

They had knocked down the wall of four cells to convert them into one much larger cell.

It was just like a dormitory. I moved in that morning and we went outside for an hour's exercise. You had to walk around in twos. It was so monotonous.

Lenny came up to me and we walked together. I told him that when my mate visited again, I would get him to bring in some Scotch. I told Lenny not to tell anyone, as you couldn't trust some of the cons.

On Monday we were back at work, with a different screw in charge.

I heard a voice call out and when I looked round, it was my mate with a parcel standing by the fence. The way was clear, so I went over to the fence.

"It's OK, Len, the screw's right up there watching the cons work."

I said they would be back soon because I was making their tea.

He gave me the parcel saying, "There's some tobacco, cigarettes, grub, bottle of scotch, bottle of brandy, some vodka and lemonade. Send me your next VO and me and the wife will pay you a visit next time."

I bade my farewells to my mate, dug a hole in the ground, and buried the stuff.

The screw came back with the cons. I took a couple of the cons who I could trust to one side and told them to make an excuse to the screw and then come back and have a drink.

When we got back to the nick I gave Davey and Lenny some tobacco, booze and fags.

About half past ten that night, we could hear someone singing at the top of his voice.

We all heard the screw shouting out, "Shut that fucking noise up or you will go down the fucking block."

Of course it was Lenny, the singing waiter. He had got himself half-pissed.

I sent my VO out to my mate the next morning and it was work as usual. We had a good week and the screw turned out to be very fair. I had my usual Saturday walk around with Lenny. He told me he got himself half-drunk and he thanked me for the tipple.

My mate and his wife came up on the visit and he told me

everybody had sent their regards and wished me luck. We had an enjoyable visit and I thanked them for coming.

By now I had done six months. Lenny the singing waiter had gone home, having done his time. I was on a Governor's call up so I couldn't go out that Monday.

When I went before the Governor, he informed me that I would be leaving Pentonville in the morning. They were sending me to Ford Open Prison in Sussex, which was for category C inmates, meaning they were low risk and not considered violent.

I arrived there on Tuesday about two o'clock in the afternoon. I went through the same routine they had in a closed nick.

First you had a bath, then you went to the stores to collect your prison clothing, then you were allocated a cell. You were told to be on Parade Square when you heard the bell and to be smartly dressed.

I thought, How can you be smartly dressed in prison gear? Me and the other inmates were on Parade Square when we were told that we would be seeing the Governor. We were all marched up to the Governor's office and called in one at a time.

He gave us the same old story about being in a closed nick. "Behave yourself while you are here, do what you are told and we will all get along fine."

We were taken to our huts, told to put our belongings away, and set our bedding the same way the other cons in the hut had theirs. Right away I thought it was just like being back in the army.

I was lying on my bed when all the other cons came in from work. They love to see a new face and to tell you what you have to do. I never asked any con what they were in for as it was none of my business.

21

i'm here
again
in an open
prison

THE BELL WENT. It was teatime and everybody rushed to be first in the queue.

It was a change from eating in your cell. Everyone had a choice of three meals and each hut had their own table to sit at.

Mind you the food was a hundred percent better than the food in the closed nick, but you still had cons moaning about it. To me it was like walking out of a one-star hotel and stepping into the Hilton. I thought the food was marvellous.

The next day it was the same old thing, see the doctor, see the welfare, see the priest and finally the prison governor.

We were all lined up and one at a time we went in. My turn came. I knew he had all my reports in front of him because they had been transferred from Pentonville.

While I stood there in front of him his glasses were half way down his nose. He looked down and then he looked up, and finally he said to me, "I can see you have a mind of your own. That's all very well, I admire that, but while you are here, fall out of line and you will be straight back to Pentonville. Do I make myself clear?"

"Yes, sir."

"Your hut will be without a cleaner next week. I have had many applications for the job, but I consider you the best man for the position. What do you say about that?"

All I could say was "Thank you, sir," although I didn't know at the time what he was talking about.

I went to the hut, then to the canteen for my meal. Then I went back to the hut and lay down on my bed. A con came in and told me I was not allowed to lie on my bed until everyone was banged up. That was when the night screw checked to make sure you were all accounted for.

I told the cons, "You had better be nice to me because from Monday I am your new hut cleaner."

It was the best job in the camp — half an hour's work in the morning and I was finished for the day. There were two blocks in Ford: A Block and B Block. A Block consisted of a brick building. You had to be over forty to get over there. Everything was inside — television rooms, snooker tables and the dining hall. Some cons even had their own single room with a light over the bed. It really was like a four-star hotel. B Block was very different. They had wooden huts, the television rooms were outside, the dining hall was outside, and you had 18 cons to a hut.

There was always a bent screw that would get you anything you wanted. For instance, there was a little Jewish guy in A Block. He had his own room and had cons running all over the place for him for a price. I'd been in his room and had strawberries and cream and even smoked salmon, and he would walk round the nick smoking his big fat cigars.

Ex-Old Bill who had strayed onto the wrong side of the law were also in the open prison. For instance two Old Bill came in while I was at Ford. One was doing six years and the other was doing seven. They put one in the visitors' room making tea for the cons and their visitors.

He could drink tea all day. The other one they put in the administration office. I had to go in there one day and he was just sitting there having his coffee and biscuits and watching his colour telly. He had his own key and he used to go over there at night-time with his bottle of scotch and watch his telly.

That's the trouble with open prisons. There is too much discrimination going on and it causes ill feelings among the cons. For some cons it's not about doing time, it's just one big long rest.

Me and two of my mates had some clothes hidden in the churchyard next to the nick. When you had your tea you could roam around the nick as you pleased until nine o'clock. You could go and watch telly or you could go down to the sports ground to play football or many other sports. We used to get under the wire, put our old boiler suits on over our uniforms and go down to the pub for a drink. We were in the pub on one particular occasion, when we got talking to this old boy.

"I can tell you boys come from London by your accent," he said.

I replied, "Yes we do. We're working in Littlehampton as pipe layers."

"Well I'm just finishing my leave. I've been transferred from another prison to finish my time off in Ford Prison." Well, if you could have seen our faces. We drank up and when we got outside we broke out laughing. We never went back to that pub again.

While I was in Ford I got to be good mates with a con called Ted. We were inseparable. Ted was a safe blower and we arranged to meet when we both got out. Prisons really are a breeding ground for crime. He lived on the other side of London so we would not have met unless we had been banged up.

He told me he had a job lined up up north when he got out. He wanted me to do the climbing and open the place up, and he would blow the safe. I agreed to this and we left it at that.

Ted was released that October. He had done his time and we had a party for him in our hut the night before he left. Most of us got half-pissed but we all had a good time and we did him proud.

I went with him to the gate the next morning to see him off.

"I will write to you, but don't write back as I will put a false address on the letter. All your letters are censored and listed by the prison officials."

The prison was getting ready for the Christmas show. I was helping out with the stage props, and we had some minor celebrities coming in to do their acts. The best acts came from the cons. I remember a black con. He was so good, the audience would not let him get off the stage. He finished finally after singing about six songs. Even Arthur Askey's daughter, Anthea, who was appearing in the show, would not stop clapping him.

I got a letter from Ted saying he had just come back from holiday. He had taken his wife to Acapulco and they had had a smashing time. He said he wished I could have been there with them.

If I hadn't lost ten days remission in Pentonville, I would have been out for Christmas. Still, we had a lovely Christmas dinner, consisting of roast chicken or roast turkey, pork, roast potatoes, green cabbage and cauliflower, and for desert there was Christmas pudding and white sauce or tinned fruit and custard. I bet a lot of people outside never had as much as we did. Then the screws came round and gave everybody five woodbines each. With all that, you still had some of the cons moaning — you just can't please some people.

We had a good governor at the time and he made it a rule that you could go to the reception a week before you were discharged to check your civilian clothes and see if they needed washing or your suit needed cleaning.

I nearly died when I opened my box. Inside there was a dirty old coat and trousers and a filthy pair of boots. I called over the prison officer in charge and told him that I had the wrong box, but he said, "It must be yours — it's got your name on it."

"When I came in here, I had a three piece suit and a pair of black shoes." I requested to see the Governor.

He took me to the Govemor's office and I explained to him what had happened.

He said how sorry he was and that they would supply me with some clothes to go out with. I said I didn't want that. So he let me make a phone call.

I rang Connie and told him my dilemma. He laughed and said, "Don't worry, I'll bring you some clothes down tomorrow."

The Governor couldn't apologise enough. I felt sorry for him and told him that it wasn't his fault. He said he would allow me a special visit tomorrow when they brought my clothes down.

At 2.30 p.m. I got called up to the visiting room and Connie was waiting for me. He had a pot of tea and told me that he had left my clothes at the main gatehouse. He said that I looked very well and asked me where I was going to stay when I got released.

"I don't know yet," I said.

"Well, I've had a word with the landlord and he said you can move back to your old room if you want to." That was a load off my mind. Connie said, "I will have all your gear back in there for when you come home."

Out of the money he had given me for the car, I would pay him the three months' rent in advance and he added, "Don't worry, I'll be at the gate to meet you when you come out!" I thanked him and as he went he said, "See you next week, son." As I was leaving the visiting room a screw told me to report to reception to check my gear.

When I got in the Governor was standing there waiting. I checked my gear and the Governor had it locked away and said he would make sure that my stuff was safe.

Some of the cons talk in telephone numbers (proper English). In there was one chap who spoke very well. He said he had a chauffeured car to pick him up when he went out. He got released the same day as me but when he got dressed he looked just like any old tramp.

He looked at me all spruced up. I didn't say anything - I didn't want to offend him.

22

my release from ford

CONNIE WAS WAITING for me outside and off we went home to Forest Gate.

As we drove through the East End I was happy to see the old place again; it was lovely. When we got home the landlord was there. He said he was sorry for my little mishap and that I should put it all behind me.

Connie had to go back to work that afternoon, so I had a bath and got myself dressed. I went to the 81 Club to see some of my old mates. They knew that I had just come out of prison, so some of them had a whip round and gave a nice few quid. That's what the people were like in the East End in those days.

On my way home I phoned Ted. He told me that the job we were going to do would not happen for a couple of months because his wife had been taken ill but he told me to keep in touch. That was the last I would see of Ted. So much for the big job!

I had been home for about three months. Now I didn't see a lot of Connie.

I was always coming and going. Later while I was living in East Ham, I was invited to a party in Wanstead. Someone I knew had had a nice little tickle, and I had done a couple of jobs with the person who was giving the party. When I got there it was packed. As soon as I was inside I had a drink placed in my hand and my mate came over to me. He told me to come and join his little crowd. He introduced me to some friends of his and we got on fine. Everybody was suited and booted, and the women were dressed well too, each trying to outdo the other.

In those days no one dressed as smartly as East End women; they really made an effort to look nice. Everybody was enjoying themselves and the drink was flowing like water.

Suddenly a very smart, good-looking man came over and put his arms around me and kissed me on the cheek. I thought this was very odd, as I didn't know him from Adam.

Then he told everybody to keep quiet. The music was turned off, and you could've heard a pin drop.

He said to me, "You don't really know me, do you?"

"No," I said.

Then he began to address the crowd. "See this little fella. He and Jack the Hat came to Dartmoor jail when I was in there and dropped me a joey."

At that moment I knew who he was—Smith from Hoxton. Everyone cheered, shook my hand and patted me on the back. He took me outside and gave me a roll of money, insisting that I take it.

I did a job with a couple of mates of mine. It was a jump-up. When we got our money, me and my mate went to Majorca for a week. We stayed in a place called Callamayour. The hotel was first class and we had a good holiday.

When I got home Connie told me that he was moving out as he was going to live with a young lady he had been seeing. I didn't want to stay there on my own, so I took the flat in East Ham.

I was doing some work for someone I thought was a mate of mine, who had a small scrap yard in Poplar. He owed me some money that he wouldn't give me. I found out he had some bags of copper in his yard one night, so I borrowed a van, broke his door open and nicked his copper. I thought I'd hold on to it until I got my money. Evidently someone who knew me had seen me and told the bloke. The next morning two police officers came to see me. They told me that he had been to see them and demanded my arrest.

When I told them why I had done it, they said, "Don't worry, we will go and see him to see if he will drop the charge. But we will have to take you to the station."

They took me to Poplar police station, put me in a cell and went to see him. When they came back, one of the officers said, "We're sorry but he wants you charged."

I came up at Arbour Square Magistrates' Court the next

morning and the judge gave me nine months because of my past record.

That afternoon I was taken to Pentonville Prison and did six months. Many of my old friends were still in there and it was as if I had never been away. I got three months off for good behaviour.

When I got out I went to see an old friend of mine, Connie Nunn. I knew all his family well, they were very nice people, and I told him what had happened. He told me that his wife had left him and I could live with him.

We got a cab and went to East Ham for my belongings. He was a good mate to me. He was straight and he let me come and go as I please.

We were having a drink with Sammy Lewis one night in a pub called The Globe. Connie went to play cards and a mate of mine came in with his wife.

Sammy had to see his wife over the road in the Blackhorse pub, so I said I would see him tomorrow. I stayed until the pub shut and went home.

I went round to Sammy's flat the next day. His wife, Vera, opened the door and she seemed very nervous.

"What's wrong?" I said.

"Haven't you heard?" she replied. "Sammy's in the Jewish hospital."

"What's wrong with him?" I asked.

She said they were walking home from the pub last night and as they were walking along Whitehorse Lane, a car suddenly pulled up and out jumped Ronnie Kray. He got

Sammy up against the wall and stabbed him in the stomach.

She asked if I would go and see him. I went straight away. He showed me the wound and while I was talking to him the police arrived and asked me who I was. I said I was a friend but before they could ask me anymore I was gone. No way did I want to get involved in a police investigation.

I went back to Vera. She asked me why Ronnie Kray would do that to Sammy. "He wouldn't hurt a fly," she said.

I had known Sammy a long time and he had never had a fight. Everybody liked him. If he had a penny, you could have half. He was that sort of bloke, always laughing. Everybody thought it was a right liberty Ronnie had taken.

In the East End in the sixties all the crooks were out to earn a bob or two. But no one did it with such ferocity as the Kray twins.

A lot of people lost what respect they had for them because of what they did to people. By that I mean cutting, maiming and killing people, running their protection rackets and terrorising everybody.

Wives lost their husbands, children lost their fathers because of the twins.

The Krays made a lot of money by targeting thieves who grabbed a few bob, even some of their own firm. A lot of people in the East End were calling them thieves and ponces. I want people to know the truth. I'm fed up of reading what good chaps they were and that Ronnie was a gentleman. I want to say to all those people and celebrities wherever you are — if the Krays had done to someone in your family what they did to many other people, would you still feel the same about them? I don't think so.

How would you feel if one night you opened your door and in front of you was your husband, brother or son standing there with his face sliced open. Or with wounds from a shooting or a stabbing. Or with a face which had been burnt with white-hot steel pokers. And don't tell me anyone deserved the punishment they meted out. What had I done to deserve the branding?

I know I was no angel, but I never used violence. No one in the East End knew what I was doing because I usually worked by myself, and it was easier in those days to hide your ill-gotten gains. Then, you could open a bank account and no questions were asked, although sometimes I used more traditional means to hide my money, like under the mattress. After one job I had forty thousand quid. I kept it all indoors at my home. The trouble was, I used to think the money would never go. I have had publicans look after some money for me. I would go into pubs and the guv'nor would hand me money. Everyone would think the guv'nor was lending me money, but really he was just giving me my own cash back that he had been keeping for me.

23

a tickle
one night
in the
west end

ME AND MY mate Sam went to the West End on information that we had received from a good friend. Only mugs did a job without information. Sam and me had a duplicate set of keys to the shop that we were going to rob, which was off Oxford Street.

The job that we had in hand was heavy work involving carting, so we got another two pals of ours to give us some assistance. They were only too glad to come along to earn themselves a few quid and they knew that if me and Sam were involved, they would be onto a good earner and it was a hundred percent. I can mention Sam's name as nobody can hurt him now, because he has since passed away. I must give full credit to him; he was one of the best key-makers that I had ever come across during my life of crime.

Everything was set. We borrowed a large van from a good friend of ours (for a price), and made our way to the West End. The van was parked, and I was the one to keep an eye on the shop until closing time. The first to come out were the shop assistants and then finally the manager. I followed him to his car, and watched him drive away. I then went back to Sam and our two friends that were waiting in the van and told them that all was clear and the shop with all its contents was ours for the taking. We put on our white coats and pulled up outside the shop we were going to rob. Sam was first out of the van and with his set of twirls started opening up the shop. Once Sam had the doors open we went to work. They went into the shop and started to gather up all the most expensive clothing. I stood outside by the van in a white overall, with paper and board in my hand, checking the goods that we were going to load onto the van. People that were walking by would take no notice of a van being loaded up that early in the evening. It took about an hour-and-a-half to load all the stolen goods onto the van. When that was done, the chaps we had got to help us got a train and went back to the East End. It wouldn't look so good to see four blokes in a van at about eight o'clock in the evening, especially through the West End. Once they were gone, me and Sam discarded our white coats and rubbing our hands together said, "It's been a good earner."

Sam by now was settled in his seat with me in the driver's seat. I said to Sam, "Right, let's get this lot in and get our dough." To our surprise, as I started to turn the engine over, nothing happened. So I tried again and again - nothing. "I don't believe this," I said to Sam. "We've slogged our guts out, come out of it clean, and now the fucking motor won't start."

There was me and poor old Sam sitting in this van with about fifty grand's worth of gear on board, stuck in the middle of the West End. I got out of the van and got the bonnet up so I could look at the engine. While I was doing this I felt a tap on my shoulder, and standing right behind me was the Old Bill. He was one of the biggest coppers I had ever seen.

"Hello," he said to me. "Having a spot of bother?"

I looked at him in amazement, and replied, "Officer this is just my luck. I've got to be in Manchester by the morning and I won't get there without a push."

With that he said, "If that's all you need that's not a problem."

Then he stopped a couple of blokes that were walking by and got them to give us a push. I got back into the van and Sam said, "What the fucking hell is going on?"

I told him that they were going to give us a push to try and start the engine. Sam looked at me in amazement. "I must give it to you, Len. I don't know what you've said to them, but you have got some fucking balls."

The police officer shouted out from the back of the van. "Contact, lads."

And off we went. Sam by now was pissing himself laughing. Here we were with fifty grand's worth of stolen goods and getting a police escort. I put the van in second gear and after about fifty yards; the engine came to life and me and Sam went off with our loot. When I looked back out of the driving mirror, all I could see was the copper's helmet rolling along the road and the copper flat out in the middle of the road. We got back to the East End, delivered the load and got a down payment on it when all the goods had been checked. We returned the van and went to meet our two associates that were involved in the crime. After we had had a couple of drinks we explained to them what had happened. Well, after telling them about the Old Bill they just burst out laughing and one of them said, "I've always said that you can always rely on an old English Bobby to get you out of trouble. God bless him. And drink up lads."

24

the
easy wage
snatch

OUR NEXT JOB was a doddle. We had to follow a chap who would drive to the bank and collect the firm's wages. At the same time each Friday morning, out he would come from the factory, give or take a couple of minutes. And we would follow him to the bank, wait for him to come out with the firm's wages, then follow him back to the firm.

This we did on a few occasions, until one Friday he changed his routine. He came out of the bank and instead of putting the bag of money in the front of the car, he opened the boot and put the bag in there. He left the bank and took a different route, not the one he took regularly every Friday morning. "That's weird," I said to my mate, "he's changed his routine.

Nevertheless, we followed him to see what he was up to. He finally stopped outside a house. He got out of the car leaving the bag of money in the boot. We watched him ring the bell. A woman came out and he went in with her. We waited to see what he would do next. We timed him while he was inside — about three-quarters of an hour. Out he came, got in his car, waved to the woman, and away he went. We followed him back to the factory and then off we went. On the way home I said to my mate, "That's strange, why did he change his routine?"

So once again, we followed him to the bank and once again he put the bag of money in the boot and off he went. Right away we knew that he was going back to the same house as the week before. We parked up and watched him ring the doorbell and go in. By now, we knew that this was not where he lived, and we found out that she was his bit on the side. So we decided that we would have the money.

I was behind the wheel of the car, and with a bunch of keys that we had, my pal made his way to the chap's car. I watched him try a couple of keys, and, bingo, the boot was open. I saw my pal lift the bag of money out, close the boot again quietly and walk back to our car. He slung the bag in the back of our car and I casually drove away. I could not believe that a man carrying a few thousand pounds could be so stupid as to leave the money in the boot, just to see his bit on the side. Some people get so confident they don't realise or think that anything could happen to them.

We went back to my pal's flat where we cut up the money.

He went his way and I was off to Jersey for a good fortnight's rest. I found out later on that the firm now sends four men to collect their money. I always thought that it was their own fault for sending one man on his own to collect that amount of cash. Still, we never hurt anybody, and after all — it was only money. I would have loved to see the look on his face when he opened the boot. How the hell did he explain that away?!

25

tony lambrianou and ronnie bender

TONY LAMBRIANOU IS the one man I cannot understand. I appeared with him on a Central Television show in Birmingham just after Ronnie Kray had died. The programme was hosted by Nicky Campbell and was titled The Krays. Its theme was whether Reggie Kray should receive parole and be set free.

Tony sat on that stage and made himself look foolish throughout most of the programme with the audience laughing and ridiculing him at the things and statements he was coming out with. He started off by saying that Reggie Kray had served his time because he had been in prison for twenty seven years and had never complained once. But by Reggie Kray's own admission, he had been involved many times in fights with the screws. Plus he was a cold-blooded killer, so what did he have to complain about?

Tony then went on to say to the women in the audience that Reggie wouldn't hurt them, he would protect them—how I don't know. He then went on to say that the reason that Reggie Kray killed Jack 'The Hat' McVittie was because Jack had challenged the Krays. Yet on a more recent programme about Reggie Kray, *The Final Word*, Tony changed his tune. When he was asked about the Krays, he changed his story and said that, in his opinion, the Krays did not know what they were doing.

Tony knew what he was saying alright because, like so many others that I have appeared with on different television programmes, they are all trying to make a name for themselves. Tony tries to give the impression that he is a gangster, which he will never be.

Even Reggie Kray calls Tony a grass in one of his books. Reggie went as far as to say that Tony was no friend of his when he did a story for a national newspaper. That is why Tony never went to see Reggie as he lay dying in the hotel in Norfolk, Reggie would not allow him to visit him.

Chrissie Barry said on *The Final Word* that Tony was the Judas of the plot and it was because of Tony that Jack the Hat was not alive today. He was fully aware of what Jack's fate was to be and he never had the guts to tell his own brother Chrissy, who went to prison for it for 13 years.

Why did Tony persist for all these years in calling for their release knowing full well that the Kray twins hated his guts? Was it because he just wanted to get back in their good books and make a name for himself? I have known the Kray twins for over fifty years, and I know that they have both slagged him off, although for a very good reason. I have known the twins much longer than Tony has because he was only taken aboard their firm after they killed Jack the Hat. I can recall poor old Billy Exley saying to me that the Krays didn't trust the Lambrianous. Why they didn't, I honestly do not know because I never knew the Lambrianous myself. As for Chrissy Lambrianou, he has now moved to the countryside, put the past behind him and is doing a very good job helping drug addicts to go straight. I must admit that I really do admire him for all the good work he is doing now. I travelled to Oxford a number of times to meet him. I always take people as I find them and to me he seemed like a nice bloke. He told me that he didn't want to speak to his brother Tony again because Tony thinks that he is a gangster.

I thought to myself, Well its alright thinking, but being one is a totally different kettle of fish. I for one wouldn't want to have to rely on the likes of him to protect me, knowing how he helped the Kray twins to set up Jack the Hat, and stood there as Reggie tore Jack's body to pieces, plunging the knife into the poor man's body repeatedly. Yes Jack was a villain, but no matter what he was, he didn't deserve to die in that most gruesome and horrible way. If Jack could have encountered Tony Lambrianou in a one-on-one situation, Tony would have shit himself.

I know Tony got 15 years for his part in the Jack McVitie trial, but I am pleased that he has got himself some money from his books since his release. I say good luck to him and his brother, Chrissy. Like another member of the Kray gang, Ronnie Bender, they never had a tanner out of the Krays after all the time they served.

I knew Ronnie Bender, a key member of the firm for about 40 years. He was a very pleasant type of bloke, good-looking and ex-army. I used to see him a lot around the spielers, pubs and clubs in the East End, and I must admit that I was shocked to discover in the 1960s that he was Ronnie Kray's driver.

I knew Ronnie Bender idolised Ronnie Kray because he was his driver for the last nine months of their freedom. What I knew about Ronnie Bender was that if he could not do you a good turn, he would not do you a bad one. He was very well liked and respected. He had been a straight man until he got himself involved with the Kray twins. He had never been in any kind of trouble with the police; he was a happily married man with three young children.

I still see Ronnie Bender even though he used to be Ronnie Kray's driver all those years ago. I meet him nearly every day and after all we have been through, we are still the best of mates.

He kept his mouth shut and what did he get from the Krays? They even state in one of their books that he was a Judas and a grass, and here is a man who had done 18 years of a 20-years sentence for the twins, and they didn't even have the decency to acknowledge him for it. No honesty among thieves — no decency either.

26

how
the krays
destroyed
lives

GEORGE CORNELL and Jack the Hat are the two best-known victims of the twins, but they ruined many other people's lives as well.

In the mid-1960s I knew a little East End Jewish fellow who had two children, a boy and a girl. He was a good man, quiet and hard-working. At the time he was working in a betting office near the Green Dragon pub in Whitechapel. Everybody liked him because he was always willing to help people, to do them a good turn. He was a straight man and someone who didn't deserve to be mucked around.

I hadn't seen him for a couple of weeks but when I did, he was a changed man. I could tell by just looking at him that something was wrong.

"Is your family all right?" I asked him.

"Yes, Len, they're OK — for the time being," he replied ominously.

"What do you mean by that? Look mate, if it's money troubles you've got, I could lend you some. I've just had a nice tickle and you can pay me back when you can."

Then he began to pour his heart out, telling me, "Len, I have to tell someone because if I don't, I think I will go off my head."

I looked at him feeling sorry for him. "Look," I said, "we all have our problems from time to time, but in the end we get over them."

"Yes, we do, as long as it doesn't involve the Krays."

I asked him what on earth he could possibly have done that meant the Krays had the needle with him.

"I could understand it if you were a villain, but you being a family man — how on earth could they have it in for you?" He told me that Ronnie Kray had asked him to look after a parcel of gold watches for him. As he was considered straight and honest, Ronnie believed he could be trusted. He told me that he hadn't wanted to do it, but at the same time he was terrified of refusing a request from the Krays, so he agreed to do as he was asked.

More than anybody, I knew how he felt but he wasn't on his own as far as the Krays were concerned. Nearly everyone in the East End was frightened of them.

So I said, "Well, if that's all he wants you to do, it doesn't seem such a bad thing, and on top of that they will give you a few quid for your trouble."

I told him not to mention it to anyone else as the Krays had their spies out, who would report back to them if anyone was saying anything bad about them.

I didn't see him for another week and when I did I couldn't believe it was the same man.

"Lenny," he said. "I've got to talk to you, I don't know what to do."

I could see he was terrified for his life. So I agreed to meet him after he had finished work.

I pulled up outside the betting shop and he got into my car.

I drove to Victoria Park. We got out and he told me that two men had conned him out of the watches. When he described them I knew that they were on the Kray firm. So the Krays had got their goods back, but still wanted him to pay for the gear.

He told me they had threatened him and his wife. I wanted to help him get out of this mess, but I didn't have the sort of money he needed. I told him not to tell anyone what he had told me.

Then I added, "To be quite honest, I don't want to be involved." The last thing I needed was another run-in with the Krays.

I dropped him off and I felt so sorry for him. He looked a wreck.

That was the last time I saw him. I had to go away for a couple of months and when I came home, I was stunned to find out he had taken his own life. I know it was because he was terrified of the Krays. Fear was how the twins forced people to do things for them.

It was such a waste of life. He was only a little family man with a wife and two kids, hard-working and never having done a wrong thing in his life until the Krays got their claws into him.

So often you hear people saying that the Krays only hurt their own. But that is absolute nonsense — they hurt anybody for money and they didn't care who it was or who they hurt. That's why they reigned in the East End underworld for so long.

One incident happened one night in a West End club, called The Merry Go Round, in Denman Street, W1. An old pal of mine was in partnership with another East End face. Their field of business was the catering side of the club.

On the night in question, customers were being welcomed into the club. We were having a drink and enjoying each other's company when into the club came the Kray twins with their entourage. After a short time one of our old East End friends, Brian Scully, who incidentally was a good thief, went out to use the toilet, followed closely by Reggie Kray. We were unaware of this until we heard screams coming from the toilet. We later learned from Brian that some weeks earlier he had taken a young lady out and there had been a disagreement. Brian had asked her to leave his car.

She was in the club on this particular night and had mentioned the incident to Reggie whom she knew. In response, Reggie gave Brian a terrible beating in the toilet and left with his group. My pal and I immediately ran to the toilet where we found Brian in a bloody heap on the floor. His face was black and blue and severely swollen. We took him to the Metropolitan Hospital in the East End, where we told the doctors that Brian had fallen down the steep staircase of The Merry Go Round. Some years later, Brian was found at his place of work, an upholstery company, where he would sometimes stay all night to fulfill an order, with his throat cut. As far as I know no one has ever been apprehended for his murder. His death was bandied around the East End and a number of conclusions were drawn as to who the murderers were. It was generally believed and accepted that the incident was the work of the Krays. Brian was a very nice, non-violent man, and I was privileged to have known him as a friend.

One man who didn't give tuppence for the Krays was George Cornell. He became such an embarrassment to them that Ronnie got himself all pissed up and blew George's brains out.

All sorts of reasons and excuses have been aired for the killing of George Cornell in March 1966. One popular theory is that Cornell called Ronnie Kray a big fat poof. Other people claim Ronnie did him because Cornell had wandered into the centre of the Krays' manor. But Cornell frequently graced the East End with his presence and was a regular drinker in the pub where he met his end. On that fateful night, 9th March, Cornell had been drinking in the Blind Beggar with Albie Woods and John Dale. Because it was a quiet night the barmaid kept playing the same song by the Walker Brothers — 'The Sun Ain't Gonna Shine Any More'.

Ronnie Kray walked in accompanied by Ian Barrie. Cornell offered to buy Ronnie a drink, but Ronnie obviously wasn't in the mood for a knee's-up. He pulled out his gun and shot Cornell three times at point-blank range. He died later that night in a hospital in Maida Vale.

Jack 'The Hat' McVitie was of the same mould as George Cornell, so they butchered him to death. Not very gentlemanly behaviour at all.

27

wandsworth

COME 1966, I was once again behind bars; this time in Wandsworth Prison doing three years for burglary. By now I was an old hand at serving my time. Mind you, I was never as experienced as some.

'Mad' Frankie Fraser has become notorious for his life of crime and has spent more than half his long life inside. He was at Wandsworth while I was there. He was inside after the great police bust of the Richardson gang in South London. The other prisoners and the screws were wary of him, to say the least.

At Wandsworth there was an area known as the Centre, which contained an office for the prison officers. The prison wings completely surrounded the Centre. No one was allowed to walk across the Centre. If you wanted to visit someone on the other side of the prison in a different wing, you had to walk right around the prison. You were expressly forbidden to walk across the Centre.

Only one man did without incurring any punishment. That was Frankie Fraser, of course. Mind you, he did it with the aid of a walking stick. At the time he was suffering injuries incurred in the infamous battle at Mr Smith's nightclub in south London.

I had a heart attack while inside after serving about eighteen months. I was released from the hospital wing and then put in C Wing. I had to go to the sick bay every morning for my medication. On one particular morning I went to my cell because I was told to rest, so I was allowed to lie on my bed in the cell. When I looked on my table I saw an envelope. I got up and read the letter contained in the envelope and had the shock of my life. The note said that if anyone came to see me I was to keep my mouth shut or they were going to shoot my two children. It was signed with a big R.

I thought I was going to have another heart attack. I knew the two cons that were in the cell opposite me, Terry and Lofty. They were the landing cleaners and they were just going to have a cup of tea. I walked in a daze to the landing, holding onto the rail. One of the cons, worried by my appearance, asked, "Is everything all right, Len?"

He helped me to his cell. I sat down and told him and his cellmate who had joined us that I had just come out of hospital and found this letter in my cell.

"Is it bad news?" said the con called Lofty. I said nothing, and they looked at me as if I had gone mad.

Terry gave me a cup of tea. "Do you want to talk about it, Len?"

I just sat there, I didn't know what to do, and Lofty added, "Look, Len, if we can help you in anyway we will."

So I gave Lofty the letter. When he had finished reading it, he gave it to Terry.

Terry asked, "What's this all about?"

The only explanation I could think of was that it was sent by the Krays and I told them what Ronnie Kray had done to me in Esmerelda's Barn.

In utter astonishment, Lofty said; "Do you mean to tell me that he did that to a little fella like you, just because you called a girl 'love'. The bastard."

He paused then and turned to Terry.

"Terry, take your shirt off and show him what the Krays did to you."

Terry did as he was asked and took his shirt off.

I just couldn't believe my eyes — he had terrible scars all over his body.

"That's what the bastards did to me," explained Terry.

I sat there just thinking about those scars. I looked Terry in the face. "Were you in bed when they did that to you?" I asked.

He looked at me with a perplexed expression on his face.

"Yes," he replied. "How did you know that?"

I told him that one night years ago I had gone to the

Kentucky Club to have a drink and as I got out of my car, the two minders who were standing at the door went inside. I went in the bar and Ronnie and Reggie were at the other end of the bar. I had had a couple of drinks when Reggie came over to me.

"Have you got a car outside, Len?" he asked.

No way was I going to say no since the minders had seen me getting out of my motor not so long ago.

Reg continued. "We're all going to a party and we ain't got enough cars. Could you take some of them in your car?"

"OK," I tersely replied. As if I had any choice in the matter!

The Kray firm came out of the club and got into a series of cars, including mine.

I was instructed to follow the cars in front.

As we were going along I piped up, "I can only stay for one drink. I've got to meet someone later." I was told that would be all right.

When I pulled the car into a street some of the chaps were already getting out of their cars and standing on the steps.

As we reached the top of the steps, Ronnie Kray turned round and barked, "We all here?"

Then he turned round and kicked the front door in. Some party this was turning out to be. Perhaps the Krays didn't have an invite and we were rather forcefully gate-crashing the event. As they all rushed in my feet left the floor and I was swept along in the rush. We all found ourselves in one of the bedrooms. I could hardly see what was going on at first. I heard this voice call out and saw a figure move on the bed. Then the mayhem really started. The Krays were stabbing this man, cutting him with razors. Ronnie had a bayonet. The poor chap was still in bed and there was blood everywhere.

I edged my way to the door and while they were all shouting I got away. When I got in my car I was shaking so much I couldn't press the clutch in at first to put it in gear. Finally I got the car moving. As I was going along I kept saying to myself, "He's got to be dead," and I could be done for being an accessory.

I shot round to my home, stuffed some clothes in a bag, grabbed some money I had hidden, and I went off. I went to a friend of mine who lived in Essex. I told him that I had to lie low for a while. I told him it looked bad.

He wasn't the type to ask you any questions, and I never told him what had happened. Every day I looked through the papers and watched the television news expecting to see or read about a murder, but I never saw or heard anything.

All I could do was pray to God that the man wasn't dead.

I stayed at my friend's for about four months. The attack never made the papers.

Terry got up and put his arm around me and said, "Don't worry. You did nothing wrong. You are always welcome in my Peter."

Then the two cons asked me what I was going to do about the letter threatening my children.

I turned to Lofty and said, "What can I do?"

I was scared, not for myself but for my children. I knew what the Krays were capable of doing.

Lofty said, "Well if they were my kids I would do something about it. Ask to see the Governor and show him the letter. Tell him what you have told us and ask him if there is anything he could do about it."

It seemed sensible advice.

I went to the landing and spoke with the prison officer, asking him if I could see the Governor right away, telling him it was a matter of life and death. He asked me what it was all about, not really believing me.

"I'm sorry, but it's personal," I replied.

He told me to go back to my cell and he would see what he could do.

After a short while the chief prison officer came into my cell and asked me what it was all about. I told him the whole story.

He told me to lock my cell, he would be back soon. True to his word he came back with the Governor who told me that he had been in touch with Scotland Yard and that someone was coming to see me. In the meantime he was going to take me out of the wings and have me transferred to the hospital where I would be put into a single cell.

I later read, in one of the many books about the Krays, that Leslie Payne, a key Kray man who had turned against them, had tipped off the police that I could be a witness against the Krays. In his book, Nipper Read wrote that we met for the first time at the Embankment, but the first time

I met him was in prison.

I now decided to give evidence against the Krays because of the note threatening my children. I assumed that the hand-written note was written outside and smuggled inside by a con sympathetic to the Krays. No one ever asked me if I had received a note.

It read: 'Keep your mouth shut. We have people watching your kids. Say no more. You know who.'

The next day, I was ordered out of my new cell and taken to an office.

Police officers Henry Mooney, Nipper Read, Frank Cater and Algie Hemmingway were all there. Nipper Read said, "What's this all about? Funnily enough, we have been looking for you."

"Well, you haven't looked very far," I replied. "I've been in prison for the last eighteen months."

They said they had come from their headquarters at Tintagel House in Vauxhall. All of them listened patiently to what I had to say. After I had finished my tale about the letter I had found in my cell and my suspicions about who may have sent it, they began to speak. They said that they already knew all about me and told me not to worry — they would see to it that my children would be protected 24 hours a day.

I asked them what was going on but they said that they couldn't say anything at the moment and that someone else would be coming in to see me.

The Governor told me that I would stay where I was for

222

the time being but shouldn't mention the visit from the police to anybody, even to people I trusted.

Mr Read said that the Governor had told them the whole story, and said that no one would hurt my children. He said he had been to the East End and a lot of people had given information about the Kray twins, and he had heard what Ronnie had done to me.

Then he showed me the newspaper. When I looked at it I nearly died. It said the Kray twins had been arrested that morning.

They asked me if I would make a statement against Ronnie Kray. I told them that I would have to think about that. We shook hands and they said they would be back to see me.

I was taken back to my cell. Late that night the Governor and the Chief came to see me. They had my civilian clothes and my personal property with them.

The Governor told me that after breakfast the following morning I was to put my civilian clothes on as I was going to be transferred to Eastchurch Open Prison on the Isle of Sheppey in Kent, and that the police would be down to see me.

The next morning the Governor and the Chief came to my cell. I was all dressed to go, and the Governor said I was to tell nobody about the police coming to see me. I would be taken straight to the new Governor's office of that nick because only he and the Chief would know why I was there. None of the prison screws would know anything about my importance to the case against the Krays. The Governor told me that if anyone asked, I was to tell them that I had been sent there for medical reasons because of my heart attack.

When I arrived at Eastchurch, I was taken to reception, given my prison clothes and allocated to hut number eight.

I had finished putting my gear away by the time the other cons came in from their work parties for lunch. They asked me all sorts of questions and I told them what I had been told to — that I had been sent there for medical reasons because I had had a heart attack in Wandsworth Prison.

Then we went to the dining hall to have our lunch. It was the same as in Ford; each hut had their own table. The food wasn't as good as Ford but it was still a lot better than a closed nick.

We got back to our hut, but all they kept talking about was the Krays getting nicked, and because I had come from the East End, they asked me if I knew them. I replied that I had heard of them, but I didn't know them. Most of them called the Krays 'wicked bastards', but a few felt sorry for them.

I was called up the following morning to see the Governor who told me that he had allocated me a light job on a garden party, and that I would be having a visit from the police that morning in the visitors' hut. I went back to my hut to change my clothes, and a screw came in.

He said, "Your name Hamilton?"

I replied, "Yes, sir."

He told me to make my way to the visitors' hut because I had a visit.

When I arrived I sat at the table where Mr Nipper Read, Mr Cater and Mr Hemmingway were already seated.

Mr Read was blunt. "If you make a statement you won't get time off your sentence. Your children are being well protected. Nobody knows my men are there so you have nothing to fear from anyone getting to them. Now I have done my bit, I would like you to do yours. Up till now, you are the only torture case we've got. But we have had a number of phone calls from the public giving us information about the Krays."

I wrote down the statement in my own words and signed it. Before they left, Mr Hemmingway said, "Len, when you go back inside the nick, if anyone asks you why you had to see the police, tell them that it's about further charges."

They told me not to worry as everything was going well and they would be back to see me in a few days. Sure enough they returned.

They told me that they had submitted my evidence to the court, and gave me a document that read: 'To Leonard Hamilton, You are hereby ordered to attend and give evidence at the trial of Ronald Kray before the current sitting of the Central London Criminal Court, Old Bailey, London EC4, or at such other court as you may be directed. Dated 10th of July 1968. MCA 16 witness order.'

"How do you feel, Len?"

"If they hadn't threatened my children, no way would you be sitting here talking to me," I replied.

But in my heart I knew that Mr Nipper Read was genuine.

He left with the words that the next time he would see me would be at the court hearing.

"You had better hurry up then, because I am being released at the end of the month," was my parting shot. It did cross my mind that the threatening note might have been a hoax, even written by Nipper Read. It seemed a major coincidence the way he turned up to see me the same afternoon I received the note but I still believe the note was genuine and it was the work of the Krays.

I didn't worry about myself. I could only think about my kids.

But even if the police had written the note, I still did the right thing. The Krays were getting way too dangerous in the late sixties, thinking they were invincible. If I was a grass, I would have grassed them up years before, when Ronnie first branded me with that red-hot poker.

A few days went by and I was called to the Governor's office. He told me that I would be taken to Bow Street Magistrates' Court in the morning and I would be let out of my hut early. He wished me good luck.

Next morning I was taken to reception, changed into my civilian clothes and taken out to a car by two screws. As I got into the back of the car I was seated in the middle of two screws and handcuffed to both of them.

"What's all this for? You don't have to do this to me," I complained.

They said it was a precaution. As we were driving off the island I noticed a car following us. I said to them, "Do you know that since we left the nick a car has been following us?" I must admit I was beginning to feel nervous.

They said not to worry. The car behind us was our escort.

28

bow street magistrates

WE ARRIVED at Bow Street Magistrates' Court and after a short wait, we finally got out of the car. All the press were there and I was ushered inside.

Mr Read told them to take the handcuffs off me, and led me away to have some breakfast. When I was called to the dock to give my evidence, I was grilled by the prosecution council and then by Ronnie Kray's defence council. They all tried different ways to trip me up, but they never had a chance because the truth will out, as the saying goes.

As I stood in the dock, Ronnie Kray was sitting in front of me pulling all sorts of faces. Then the judge called a recess. Boy, was I glad to get out of there. I was surrounded by police and taken to a room.

Mr Read and Mr Cater came in and asked me how I felt.

"Bloody awful," I replied.

I thought I was going to collapse. I had never given evidence against anyone before in my life.

Mr Read said, "Don't worry, Len, you're doing just fine. You're doing the right thing and a lot of people will thank you for that. I know George Cornell's wife will and so would your mate Jack the Hat."

We were called back into the court and once again I was in the witness box. The judge asked me if I would like to sit down, and also if I would like a glass of water. I said yes to both questions. I think he knew that I was just getting over my heart attack.

Once my evidence was completed, the judge committed Ronnie Kray to the Old Bailey. I was led out of the dock and taken to another room. Mr Read shook my hand and all the other police were cheering. I was given a cup of tea, which was refreshing, but I wished to God that it had been a brandy.

They waited until everybody had gone, then they put me in a car. Mr Read said to the screws, "No need for the cuffs," and threw me a packet of fags. As we drove away, the same car escort followed us back to the nick.

When we arrived at the nick, I was taken out of the car and into the gate office.

The screws who were on duty at the gate said, "Blimey. What you been up to?"

The screw who had been my escort replied, "He's had a right old day."

He told them that I was a witness on the Kray case. I could not believe it — I was taken to the Governor's office, and I told him what had been said.

"Don't worry," he said. "Before it goes any further I will go and have a word with them."

But by this time it was all over the nick.
I got back to my hut. The blue band, the con who's in charge of the hut, came over to see me. "Don't worry, Len, we're all with you," he said. So I told them the whole story.

Some of them said if they'd had that done to them, they would have got a gun and shot the bastard. It's easy to talk, I thought, but it's another thing to put it into action.

I was released from Eastchurch at the end of July and as I walked out of the gate, I was met by a police car and put under police protection. That was how I was to spend the next 14 months. I was taken to a large building which faced onto the River Thames, called Tintagel House. I was driven to Mr Read's office. Above the door was the word 'Krayology'.

Mr Read was a nice man. He asked me if I was all right and said that I would soon be taken to my new address which was in Hampstead, North London. I would have two police officers with me 24 hours a day, changing over every morning.

Then I was taken to meet Mr John Durose, Mr Henry Moony and Mr Bert Trevette. Mr Trevette was a kindly man who was in charge of finding safe houses for witnesses and for their subsequent protection.

I must say that it was a thankless job for him, but I never heard that man grumble. There was nothing that he wouldn't do for you, and if he is alive today I would like to thank him for all that he did for me. I was taken to the canteen to have a meal. Whilst I was in there I saw two villains I knew. I pretended that I hadn't seen them.

Mr Mooney came to take me back to Mr Read's office and I told him whom I had seen. He said I was to forget that I had seen them as they were giving information about the Krays, but they refused to go into the witness box and do it.

I entered Mr Read's office. He introduced me to the two officers that would be with me that day, and I told him that I had to get my clothes from the East End.

"I know where it is because I've already been there," Mr Read said.

We got to Connie Nunn's house and he let us in. We shook hands and I told him what was happening. I packed my bags and got the money I had hidden before I went to prison. I gave Connie five hundred quid. He was well pleased.

We shook hands and he said, "Don't worry, Len, there's a lot of people on your side. Under the circumstances you could do nothing else."

He wished me good luck and as I went to go, he added, "Len, when it's all over you can come back and live here anytime."

"Thanks, Connie. See you when it's all over," I replied.

29

in a hampstead safe house

WE ARRIVED at a big house in Hampstead. Inside there were well-furnished, self-contained flats. I know that some of the residents must have thought it was strange because they would always see me accompanied by two men one day and another two the next. It may have been the swinging sixties, but people weren't used to that sort of thing.

We used to go to a pub called The Bull and Bush near Hampstead Heath, rather different from the pubs in the East End. It was a lovely pub and the clientele consisted of students and sightseers. Sometimes even a few stage and film stars would come in.

We had been going there for about six weeks, usually standing in the corner of the bar, when one night a young girl came up to me and said, "I've been watching you and your friends." She had had a few drinks, possible giving her the courage to talk to me. "Are you something to do with the Mafia and are these big men your bodyguards?"

"No, they are all my lovers," I replied with a straight face.

Well, if you could've seen her face. Crestfallen, she went back to her friends at their table. But ten minutes later she came back and asked, "Are they all really your lovers?"

"If you ask a silly question, you'll get a silly answer," I told her.

I got on speaking terms with the guv'nor of the pub whose name was Mr Wilson.

He was a well-dressed man and also well spoken. One night he told me that his son was a road manager of the then very popular band, The Walker Brothers. The band had broken up and Garry, the drummer, was living in the pub but was too shy to come down and meet people.

I asked Mr Wilson what he drank. Scotch, he said. So every night I used to send him up a half bottle of Scotch. One night Garry did come down to thank me. He was a really nice chap, and we had a long talk. I said to him, "Don't worry, we all have our ups and downs and everything will turn out roses in the end."

I have since read in the paper that he lives in Tilbury and is now married. I wish him all the luck in the world.

One day when we had been living in that flat for about two months, I saw a well-known villain going into a nearby flat as we were on our way out. We were going up to Tintagel

House that day and on the way I told the two officers what I had seen, but I would not tell them who it was I saw. I said that I would not give them his name or the flat that I saw him go into.

We got to Tintagel House and went in to see Mr Read. The officers told him what had happened and right away he said, "You can't stay there any longer. Don't worry about it. Go home. You will be moving tomorrow."

While we were sitting in the flat I made an excuse that I wanted some fags. One of the officers said he would go and get me some. I told the remaining officer that I was going to have a bath. The bathroom was on the landing and while I was there I wrote a note and pushed it under the villain's door, telling him that two Scotland Yard officers were living in the house.

When I got back to the flat, Mr Travette was there. "Pack your things," he said. 'I'm putting you in a hotel until I can get you a safe place to live."

That night we left and booked into a hotel in Adelaide Road in Swiss Cottage. We were booked into a room for four people until suitable accommodation could be found.

While we were there, we were still going to The Bull and Bush pub because now we were accepted and no one asked any more questions. Standing at the bar one night, a little fellow like myself came in and stood beside me. Mr Wilson came over and introduced us. His name was Dicky Henderson, a comedian of stage and screen. We were having a drink together when in walked another man, who I became great friends with. It was Ian Hendry, the film star. He had a lovely house opposite the pub, and was married to an actress called Janet Monroe. He told me that before he had got into films, he used to drive a van for a florist delivering flowers to hotels. He turned out to be a very good friend of mine and he was the only one I confided in.

One night he invited me to his house and we had a good chat. He said to me, "I can tell that you are genuine and sincere. You don't find many people like that in my kind of work." Ian said to me that when this filthy business had finished, he would like me to come back to him.

Two police officers arrived at the hotel the next morning to change over with the two who had been with me the day before. They had only been there for about half an hour when there was a knock on the door. One of the officers opened it and in came the manager of the hotel. He told us to pack our belongings and get out. He had had our room watched and seen all these different men coming and going, and he was disgusted.

"I don't let such things go on in my hotel. Get out or I will call the police."

When he had gone we sat on the beds laughing our heads off and I said to the two officers, "I didn't know you two were perverts."

The officers had been given strict instructions not to divulge who they were, so we had to leave the hotel. We went to Tintagel House and told Mr Trevette what had happened. He saw the funny side too and burst out laughing.

"Until I can find you a safehouse, would you like to come and stay at my home?"

"I don't mind as long as I'm not putting you out," I replied. His wife was a lovely woman. Her name was Sue, and she couldn't do enough for me. While I stayed there, they took one of the officers away from me.

30

a police officer's bribe

EVENTUALLY TREVETTE found me a nice flat in Potters Bar. It was on the top floor, and I only had one officer with me at a time, so the two officers took it in shifts with each accompanying me on alternate days. One of them I didn't like at all. I had a bad feeling about him from the start.

He kept asking me all sorts of questions about the Krays and people I knew. His comments and questions soon became more blatant. "Wasn't I fed up of being on the case?" and "If I could get a few thousand pounds, how would I like to disappear off the case away from it all?"

I told him that I did get fed up at times living with the police. It must have been the same for them too. What with them being away from their wives and families, we were all under tremendous strain, especially the witnesses who had their wives and children with them. Nobody could imagine what we all went through, though I give the police their dues — they did try to make things as easy as possible.

Each day when this officer came on duty, he would bring up the subject of the Krays again. I wondered what he was up to, so I just strung him along.

On the Thursday he told me he had it all arranged. He was going to take me to a party on the Saturday night where I would be given five grand to leave the Krays' case.

I said, "OK, that'll do me. I'm just about fed up with all this anyway."

He said that he had to meet some people that night, so I would be on my own for a while and I was not to go out.

I thought to myself, Things ain't right. He's here to protect me and here he is, leaving me on my own. I had known right from the start that he was a wrong 'un.

He went out of the flat and I saw him get into his car and go. All sorts of things were going through my mind.

"Is he setting me up?" I asked myself and came to the conclusion that he was.

I thought that at any minute now someone would come through that door and I would finish up dead.

I went to the kitchen, got a carving knife, and put it under my pillow. Then I made sure all the windows were shut and finally I bolted the front door. I turned out all the lights and sat by the window so I could see if any cars pulled up. I didn't get any sleep that night. It was sometime between 2 and 3 a.m. when I saw his car pull up. I quickly unbolted the door and got into bed. I heard his keys going in the lock to open the door. He came into my bedroom and started shaking me. His breath stank of drink. He asked what I had been doing. I told him that I had a headache and had gone to bed.

He said he had it all arranged. He was going to take me to a party in Crouch End on Saturday night and someone he knew would give me the money. Then we would go back to the flat. I was to pack my bags while he was supposed to be asleep, put the bags in his car, take his car keys and get away. I said to him, "Won't you get yourself into any trouble?"

He replied, "How can I? I can't watch you while I'm asleep now, can I?"

I asked him what he was doing this for, and he said "If one of the witnesses fucks off the case a lot of the others will get scared and leave too."

"If that's the case, where does that leave me?" I asked him.

"You haven't got a worry in the world. If the Krays get off this case, there is nothing that they wouldn't do for you."

He went to bed and it wasn't long before he was snoring. I made myself some strong black coffee to prevent myself from falling asleep. But I was so worked up I don't think I would have got a wink of sleep anyway. I sat by the window all night and must have smoked about fifty fags.

I couldn't wait for the morning to come; it seemed a lifetime waiting. While I was sitting there, all I could think was, What a rotten bastard.

He could wreck everything, all that the witnesses had gone through and everything that the police had done to make this all possible. I started thinking of how I used to carry the empty fish crates for George Cornell in the fish market and the times he would give me a few quid to buy my mother something. How he must have felt when Ronnie Kray pointed that gun at his head in the Blind Beggar pub before blowing his brains out. I thought of poor old Jack 'The Hat' McVitie and how he must have felt when he walked in that house in Stoke Newington, before they finally killed him. What fear and pain he must have gone through. I thought of all the other people that the Krays had sliced open, maimed, and all the people the Krays had extorted money from. No, I was not going to let all those people down.

I let the officer sleep as long as possible, because the other officer would be coming on at nine o'clock. At eight o'clock, I made a pot of tea.

When he got up he had a cup of tea and said, "Don't forget what I said. Everything is all arranged and when the other bloke comes on duty, don't you tell him anything."

"What do you take me for?" I replied. "Do you think I would pass up five grand just like that?" And just to make him feel good I said, "Here's to tomorrow night."

"That's my boy," he replied.

It was nearly nine o'clock and as I was looking out of the window, I saw my escort for the day pull up in his car. His name was Bill Laver and he hailed from Ponders End.

He had one of those German Beetle cars and he was one of the best officers that watched over me. He always thought of my personal safety. He was what we in the East End call a 'diamond'.

The bell rang. In walked Bill. He took the keys to the flat, went to the window and waited until the other officer's car had gone. Bill went into in the kitchen to make some tea. While the kettle was boiling, he went through the cupboards to see what food we had and what we needed. While he was doing that, I ran a bath.

Bill had made some toast. He cast me a quizzical look when we sat down. "You look like you've been up all night," he observed.

I looked straight at him and replied, "Would you believe it? I have."

I got dressed, then said to Bill, "I don't know what to do."

He asked, as quick as a shot, "Is it something to do with him who's just gone?"

"Yes, it's all to do with him."

"Is it something that he's done or said that's upset you? Because, Len, that's what I'm here for. I'm here to look after you and give you any help I can."

So I told him the whole story.

When I had finished he just sat there without speaking for a short while. Then he said "Len, is that the truth you've just told me?"

"Do you think that I could make something up like that? If you don't believe me, let's go round to his house and see him!"

Bill said the officer would only deny it all. He picked up the phone and rang Tintagel House. When he put the phone down, he barked, "Right, we're going to see Nipper Read right away."

We got to Tintagel House and went straight to Nipper's office. Bill told him the whole story. When he had finished, Mr Read said, "The dirty little bastard. What's he think we've been doing for the last two years — sitting on our fucking arses?"

Mr Read told Bill to take me to the canteen while he sorted this problem out.

When we went back to Mr Read's office, he said we were in luck because it was Bill's extra duty that weekend which meant that I would not see the other officer till Saturday evening at about seven o'clock. They did this on weekends. Then he said, "I want you to go back to your flat and we'll be there later on today. I've found you a lovely flat in Boreham Wood, and if all goes to plan you should be out of the flat by the weekend." Then he said to me, "I want you to go home and act normally when he comes on duty tomorrow night. Whatever you do, don't let him suspect anything and don't worry. From now on, we will be watching your flat. Mr Laver knows what he has to do, so you have no worries there."

Me and Bill left, and on the way home we did some shopping. Out of my own money, I bought some beers and a couple of bottles of spirits.

When we got in the flat, we settled down to watch the horse racing on the telly and had a couple of drinks. The phone rang. Bill answered it. When he put it down he said that Nipper and a few others were on their way to see us. They arrived about an hour later and set about putting some bugs in the flat. When they had done that, Nipper said, "Right, I want you to get him as near to the mikes as you can without raising the slightest suspicion. I want you to get him talking about the money."

When it was all set up, Mr Read left. He came back a short while later and seemed pleased. "That's perfect. We have somebody in the flat below you and they will monitor everything you say. They will stay there now until this is all over."

Then he gave me a pair of dark surgical glasses to wear and a bottle of migraine tablets, and said, "Before he comes in, I want you to wear the glasses and lie down on the settee with that bottle of tablets on a table in front of you. I would sooner put a bastard like him away than any villain. No matter what he says you must not go to that party with him. You have to play up on the migraine and as soon as he leaves I want you to pack your bags — you will be leaving here as soon as he's gone. Len, you will love the flat you are going to. It belongs to someone in the film business and if all goes according to plan I will come and see you very shortly."

Later on that day we went to Bill's home. He introduced me to his wife. She was lovely and very good-looking. What I liked about her was that she never asked me any questions. It got late and Bill said, "If you want, you can stay here tonight. My wife will make you up a bed."

I was so glad he said that, as I didn't feel safe in that flat anymore. He phoned up Tintagel House and told them where I would be that night. That was Bill — everything by the book.

He woke me up the next morning with a cup of tea, and his wife cooked us breakfast. As we left, I kissed her on the cheek, and thanked her for everything. She told me I could stay at their house anytime.

We got back to the flat and we hadn't taken our coats off when the doorbell rang. Bill shut me in the bedroom and answered the front door. Then he opened the bedroom door and let me out. It was Mr Read and Mr Cater. They said they were in the flat below and asked me if I was OK.

"Yes," I replied. "I don't know what I would have done without Bill."

They didn't stay long, but before they departed Nipper said, "Don't worry, we're right downstairs. Mind what you say now as we can hear everything." As he walked out the door he added, with a big smile on his face, "That means you too, Bill."

It was getting near the time for Bill to hand over to the other officer. Bill had put a bottle of tablets on the table and told me to lie down on the settee. He gave me the glasses to put on. Now everything was ready.

Bill looked at his watch — it was 7.30 p.m. "That fucking bastard," he said. "It doesn't look like he's going to show."

It was nearly eight o'clock when the bell rang. Bill opened the door and grunted, "You're late."

The officer walked in and took a look around the flat. He noticed the pills and asked, "What's wrong with Lenny?"

Bill said he had had to get the doctor round as I had

suffered a very bad attack of migraine. With that Bill picked up his bag and said, "I'll see you both tomorrow night. My wife will wonder where I have got to."

The officer asked me if I was all right and then he said, "What about tonight? It's all arranged. That's why I'm late. The party's going ahead and your five grand is there waiting for you to pick up."

"Look," I asked. "Can you trust this bloke who's putting up the money for me to disappear from the case?"

"No problems there."

"Can't you go to the party? I'll be OK here. I'm not going anywhere — my fucking head is killing me. You know that I had a splitting headache the other night."

I thought that would convince him, but I added, "While you're gone, I can pack my bags and be ready to go when you get back."

And to make it seem even more genuine, I said, "Make sure the car is full up with petrol as I want to get as far away from here as I can. When you come back, you had better have the money with you, otherwise it's all off."

"Don't worry, Len, I will have it. These people I'm dealing with are no mugs."

"OK. Before you go, can you get me a glass of water?"

Then to convince him even more I took a couple of tablets. He seemed to buy the story.

When he had gone, I went to the window and saw him get into his car. As he pulled away I saw two cars come from nowhere and follow him.

The police came up to the flat from downstairs. Bill was with them. He told me to pack my belongings. We were leaving, and going to a new flat — this one wouldn't be safe anymore.

We got to Boreham Wood, where I was to spend the rest of my time while I was on the Kray case. Nipper Read came to see me the next day and told me that I wouldn't be seeing that other officer any more. He asked me how I liked my new flat. I said it was lovely and it was. It was on private land well hidden by large poplar trees.

I now had two different detectives minding me on alternate days. One was a sergeant from the city police. His name was Roy, a nice man who was very smart. I think he would have made an ideal James Bond as he looked the part. The other officer's name was Eric, and he was one of the most genuine men I have ever met. He originally came from Yorkshire. He was a big broad chap who looked a typical rugby player. Being quite sensitive, he knew when you were up and when you were down, and he knew how to make you forget what you were going through.

One day we had a ride around the country and stopped in a pub in Radlett. It was only a few miles from where we lived. While we were in the pub, Eric noticed a fellow he knew who was in the force. He went over to talk to him and we all finished up having a drink together. They told me they were having a lot of problems with one of the witnesses on the case, and could I help them. I asked how.

They said they had left a WPC with a troublesome witness

while they got some shopping and then had a quick drink. They told me her name was Claire. She was a witness on the Frank Mitchell bust-out from Dartmoor. Frank Mitchell had been sprung out of prison by the Krays. Later after a campaign to have him released from his sentence, he mysteriously disappeared. The police thought the Krays had killed him. To make the witness feel better, the police were giving her a party on Friday night. They asked me to come as she said that she was getting fed up of only seeing police around her. They thought that I could come and speak to her as it might make her feel a bit better.

I said if I could be any help I would. I knew what she was going through, being in the same boat. They gave Eric their address and as they left they added, "Don't forget — Friday night."

When we got back to the flat, he said he wasn't keen on the idea. "Well, we can't let them down, can we?" I replied.
Friday came and still Eric didn't want us to go. But I was getting fed up too, so I managed to persuade him.

When we got there it was a lovely bungalow and music was playing. I knocked on the door and in we went. We were – all introduced to each other, and after we had had a few drinks, Claire said to me, "I'm glad you came."

We went into the kitchen and she told me that she was scared, and that she didn't think she would last it out. I told her that she wasn't on her own, as there were several of us trying to handle the stress of it all. She said it was nice to be able to talk to someone from the East End.

I sat talking and drinking with her for a couple of hours. I went to the toilet and as I came out, one of the officers who was looking after her thanked me for coming. "I don't know what you said to her, but she feels a lot better now."

I had told her that a lot of people in the East End had lost all respect for the Krays when they ordered the killing of Frank Mitchell. After all the bird he had done, to have to go and die like that wasn't right. And if they didn't get stopped now, there was no telling what other people would go through and what suffering they would bring to other families.

I could see that she felt a lot better after that, so we went into the living room to join the party.

We had a few drinks and she said she wanted to dance with me. She was very attractive and she had plenty of form. I thought that it was the drink that was making her seem amorous. I indicated to one of the officers to give me a rest, so he came over and asked her to dance with him.

While they were dancing I got talking to one of the other officers who was minding her and told him that she was wearing me out. I didn't want to upset her but I thought it was time for me to go. With that he went over to her and told her we were leaving.

She just walked past us all and went out of the front door and then she started running away. I didn't know what was going on but the WPC and one of the other officers ran out after me. They finally caught up with her and brought her back. They took her into the living room and I tried to calm her down.

The other officer came over to me and asked me if he could talk to me in the kitchen in private. So in we went.

He said to me, "Len, I just don't know how to say this, but I will do the best I can." He told me that he was only there temporarily, as they had had to take one of the other officers away from her to give him a rest. Apparently this officer's wife was carping on that she has not seen her husband for some time.

"What's that got to do with me?"

He told me that the officer they had taken away from her was regularly sleeping with the witness to keep her happy. Well, I looked at him and said, "You must be joking."

He said, "Len, it's no joke. We have to do it to keep her happy. After all, she is the main witness in the Frank Mitchell case. The Krays took her on trial runs to Dartmoor Prison, deciding the best way for them to get Frank out of the nick. Having a woman with them took away a lot of suspicion."

"Now that you've told me all that, what's it got to do with me?"

"She is frightened to sleep alone and she has to have someone to sleep beside her." He continued that she had told them that she liked me, and that they didn't want to upset her. I would be doing them a great favour because they couldn't afford any trouble.

I looked at him, laughed and said, "You must be pulling my leg."

He assured me he wasn't and asked me if I was prepared to help out.

I said I would but I still didn't believe him.

"I will go and tell her that you will stay the night with her. Thanks, Lenny."

I went and got myself a drink. When I told the officer who was guarding me the story, he just laughed and said that he wished they had asked him.

Claire came over to me and said, "Len, you won't regret it." All I could think was, What have I let myself in for?

By two o'clock in the morning, some of the other guests had left and Claire said to me that she wanted us to go to bed. So we did.

She finally dropped off to sleep at about 4 a.m. I gave her about half an hour of sleep then I got up and got dressed.

One of the officers was still awake. He came to the door with me and asked if I had enjoyed myself. I said to him, "What is it with her? I'm knackered."

Then he told me that she was a nymphomaniac.

"You bastard," I said, with a big smile on my face.

We shook hands and I got ready to leave.

Just as we were leaving, Claire woke up and kissed me, and thanked me for coming.

"Well, if you can't help your own, who can you help?" I replied. As we drove away she waved goodbye. That was the last time I saw her. I hope that wherever she is, she has settled down, and had a nice life. God bless her.

It was getting near the trial date. Mr Read came to see me and informed me that as I was the only torture case they had I would probably be the first to go in the witness box at the

Old Bailey. He asked me how I felt about that and I said it was okay.

He said he would come and see me in a few days' time. When he did, he said that they had changed their minds. They were now going to put the murder cases on first — the killings of George Cornell, Jack 'The Hat' McVitie and Frank Mitchell.

I was pleased that I wasn't going to be called yet, but also irritated as the whole saga had taken up so much of my life. I wanted to say my piece and get away from it all.

The Kray case dragged on. I think it must have been one of the longest criminal trials in English history. Me and the police officer Eric were watching the telly when it was announced that the Krays had been found guilty of two murders — Ronnie for George and Reggie for Jack 'The Hat' McVitie.

Then came the sentences. They were each given life with recommendations that they each serve not less than 30 years. Eric jumped out of his chair and punched the air and shouted out, "Yes!"

It couldn't have happened to nicer people.

We went to The Bull and Bush pub in Hampstead and we both got drunk. I was relieved that I was not going to be called to give evidence.

However, I did feel a bit sorry for Reggie because I think that Ronnie was the more dominant of the two and that if Ronnie had not shot George, Reggie would not have killed Jack. I phoned a friend of mine in the East End and he told me that most people were not sorry for them. He said that in the pub, people were saying, "Fuck them, they deserved everything they got."

Now came the time for the police to sort out what they were going to do for the witnesses on the case. Some went abroad with new identities and others went to live in different parts of the country, also with new identities.

Mr Read asked me what I wanted to do.

I said, "As far as I'm concerned, I think that I've done nothing to be ashamed of and after a few months I will be going back to the East End. Nobody is going to make me leave it, and I love the East End people. You will always get the odd ones who will say I shouldn't have done it. Well, that's life and they are entitled to their own opinions."

I'd been on the case now for 14 months and the police had found me a flat in Finchley Central in Etchingham Park Road. It was a private block situated in its own grounds in Etchingham Court, just around the corner from the police station. They gave me some money for food and paid three months' rent in advance. I was given a special phone number in case I ran into any trouble and that was it. After 14 months of police protection I was now on my own.

When they had gone, I went to the local off-licence and got a large bottle of brandy and some beers. It seemed strange now being on my own. But to tell you the truth, I was glad it was all over.

I had been there a couple of weeks when the bell rang and it was Mr Trevette who had come to see if I was all right. I told him that I was going to the local job centre to get a job. He left me some money for food and such, and left.

The next day I went to the job centre and asked to see the manager. I was shown into his office and I explained that I had only recently moved there. He asked me what I had been doing for the last two or three years. So I thought that I would tell him the truth.

When I explained to him what I had been doing, he went white. When he finally got his voice back, he said, "What do you want me to do?"

He said it would be impossible for him to find me anything.

I walked out of his office and went straight to the betting office opposite and backed two winners. When I went to collect my money the payer-out looked at me as if to say 'Who are you?'

He counted out my money — I had won seven hundred and fifty quid — and out I walked.

31

are you
   ever really
free ?

A COUPLE OF weeks later, I was walking down Ballards Lane. I got to the police station and saw several police officers looking out of the window. As I walked on, they came up behind me and asked me to go back to the station with them. This I did.

When we got inside they asked me what I was doing in Finchley. I told them that I lived there, and gave them my address. They said they had been keeping an eye on me.

So I said, "Well, you know my name and where I live. Now what have you got me in here for?"

They asked me what I did for a living. I replied that at the moment I was doing nothing.

They said that a jewel robbery had gone off that day and that I was being held for further enquiries. They told me to empty my pockets and when they saw the money I had on me, they said, "Not bad for doing nothing."

Then some other officers turned up. They had turned my flat over and found the money I had hidden there. They said that they were going to put me in the cells.

It was then that I gave them the phone number of Tintagel House.

I had been in the cells for a couple of hours when in came Bert Trevette. He explained to them that I had been on the Kray case and they looked dumbfounded. They gave me back my belongings and Bert dropped me off at home.

He came up to my flat and asked me how I got on with my neighbour opposite. I said that I'd only seen him a couple of times but his face was familiar to me.

"Well," he said, "you have no worries there — he was on the Kray case. He gave evidence against Ronnie Kray. He was the driver of the car that drove Ronnie to the Blind Beggar on the night he shot George Cornell." It was Scotch Jack Dickson.

I went downstairs to see Bert to his car. After he had gone, a woman called to see me. Her name was Bridie. She was Irish and lived with her two daughters and her husband, who was a black cab driver. She invited me over for a drink.

When we were inside her husband shook my hand and gave me a drink. They asked me how I liked living here, and said they had a card school and they played kalooki. Would I like to come over and play sometime, if I had some spare time on my hands?

They were a nice everyday family and we ended up very good friends. They said they were having a party on Saturday night and would I like to come over? I said, I would.

That night I went to have a drink at The Bull and Bush. Mr Wilson the landlord asked me where my friends were nowadays as he hadn't seen them for a while. When I told him who they were, he said he had suspected all along that they were police officers. So I told him the whole story. He gave me a double brandy and wished me luck. He said the Krays were now where they belonged.

After I had been in Finchley for about two months, I decided one night to go to a Joe Coral's spieler in Stamford Hill.

When I got there, there were some big rummy games being played. I got in one of the games and finished up winning a few hundred quid.

It was about 1.30 a.m. when I left. As I walked down the alley to get a cab home, four blokes jumped me and gave me a right kicking. One of them stabbed me in my right leg. As they were getting away I recognised one of them.

I got a cab home and cleaned myself up.

When I woke the next morning I felt really sore and I had bruises all over my body. I had strapped my leg to stop the bleeding.

I phoned a friend of mine in the East End and told him what had happened. He told me he would go and see the man I had recognised. He was a good pal of mine and he hated the Krays. The attack seemed senseless.

A bit later on he phoned me and wanted to me to go to the East End to meet him. I said I couldn't go out as I was injured. He said not to worry, he would come to me.

A couple of hours later the bell rang and there was my friend with one of the blokes that had set about me the night before. I let them in and gave them a drink.

My mate said, "Len, there's been a bit of a mix-up."

Then the other bloke told me what had happened. He said that they had just had it off for a nice few quid and they were all half pissed. Someone had wound them up saying I used to be with the Krays and as the Krays had shot one of the other blokes' uncle five years ago, they thought they would get a little bit of their own back. They obviously thought it was safer to hit back now that the Krays were inside for a long stretch.

When I told him the whole story he just kept saying how sorry he was and thanked me for not going to the police. If I ever came back to the East End and needed any help, he would be there for me, he said. As they were going, he gave me five thousand quid for the trouble they had put me through.

32

the offer
of a job

IT WAS A lovely summer's day. I was walking along Finchley Central when I met a Jewish chap called Ivor who I was in the nick with. He had served time for gold smuggling.

We went and had a drink, and he asked me what I was doing. When I told him I was fed up doing nothing he asked me if I would like a job driving his wife's relation.

He had a Rolls Royce and lived in Nuttsford Place, off the Edgware Road, near Marble Arch. his name was Allen Bruce Coopoer and he had also been a witness on the Krays' case. So Ivor phoned Cooper who told me to go and see him in the morning. Ivor said he would come and pick me up and take me to see him.

The following morning, on the way to see Cooper, he told

me all about him. He was a naturalised American and had been the one that had supplied guns for the Krays. He would file the firing pins down so they would not fire.

We arrived at Cooper's flat. He was a small man with a limp and he stuttered a bit. He also had a strong American accent. We shook hands and he said that he wanted a driver to drive his Rolls Royce and to manage his art shop in the West End of London.

He said he had to be careful who he trusted as the Krays had put a contract out on him. As I had also been a witness on the case, he knew he could trust me.

I went to work for Cooper. Various people would come into the shop to see me. Leslie Payne visited me there – he was also a witness on the Krays' case. Even with the Krays inside, I could not escape their influence. Sir Peter Moon and Bob Gould, whom I later worked for on the continent, also used to come in. I began to wonder what I had let myself in for, as they were all conmen, but I liked Cooper and Gould because they were good to me.

One nightCoopers phoned me and told me to pick a friend of his up at London Airport and take him to the Hyde Park Hotel, where he would be staying for a while.

A short while later I found out that he was an arms dealer. While he and his friend were on a business deal, his friend had been shot dead but he had managed to escape.

I told Coopers that I would not drive his friend about anymore, nor did I want to get involved in any shady deals. He begged me to stay as his driver as he knew he could trust me, and said that I would not have to drive any of his associates about again.

A few months went by and one afternoon he asked me to drive him to Euston Station where he had to meet someone. While we were going along I asked, "Do you feel all right?" because for the last few days he had been acting strange and seemed a bit nervous.

He said he would tell me all about it after we had seen this man at Euston Station. We arrived at the station and he told me to park. He got out of the car and I saw him get into another car along the rank. After a short while I saw him get out of the car and shake hands with a tall man whom I recognised to be a high-ranking police officer from Scotland Yard.

As he came up to me I knew something was not right. He was as white as a sheet.

He got into the car and we drove off.

He didn't say much on the way and told me to drive him to the Hilton Hotel in Park Lane as he needed a drink.

We went into the hotel, he ordered some drinks and we sat at a table.

I asked him what was wrong. He told me to go to his flat and ask his wife to pack him some bags and have them sent to the Hyde Park Hotel to his friend's room. He said he could not risk going home himself and that it was not safe for him to phone as his phone might be tapped.

I went to his flat and told his wife, Beverley, what had happened and then went back to the Hilton.

When I got there I said, "Now look, Allen, what's going on?"

He told me that the man he had met that afternoon had told him to get out of the country because the police from Chelsea Station had a warrant out for his arrest and they would be arresting him in the early hours of the morning. Also two of his associates were in need of help; one had put himself into a Harley Street nursing home and the other had placed himself in a mental home.

I said, "Allen, what have you got yourself involved in? It's not murder, is it?"

"No, it's not as bad as that, but it had all come on top with the banks."

He told me to go home and stay indoors, as he would be phoning me later that evening and not to mention it to anyone.

I waited for the phone to ring and, as it was getting late, I went to bed. I was woken up by the phone ringing. I looked at the bedside clock - it was 1.15 a.m. I picked up the phone and it was Allen. He asked me if I was alone. I said I was. He wanted me to pick him up at 5 a.m. in the morning at the Hyde Park Hotel and drive him to the airport. He had everything arranged.

I told him that I would be there on the dot. He asked me, if, when he had got settled in the States, I would like to live with him and his family in Phoenix, Arizona.

He said that he had phoned Bob Gould who was now in Paris, and he had arranged for Bob to have a plane ticket left for me at Heathrow Airport, as Bob wanted me to be his driver on the continent. The ticket would be at the airport on Friday morning.

The last words he said to me were, "Whatever you do, don't be late."

I told him that I would stay up now.

I arrived at the Hyde Park Hotel at 4.45 a.m. Allen came out with his friend and his wife at exactly 5 a.m.

When he had got his bags in the car, he said he wanted to go to Rochford Airport near Southend in Essex. When we got there, I helped him with his bags. I said goodbye and he gave me an envelope. It was pretty thick and he told me not to open it until I got home.

That was the last time I was to see Allen Cooper.

I drove his friend and his wife back to the Hyde Park Hotel. His wife told me to come to her flat in the evening. I went back to my flat in Colindale. I ran a bath and remembered the letter Allen had given me at the airport. When I opened it, it contained a letter and five hundred quid. In the letter it said that the money was for being loyal to him and for not asking any questions. He wrote that if I ever wanted to go and live with him in Phoenix in the United States, I would be most welcome.

Well, I am glad I never did go out there, as I read in the paper, a couple of years later, that he and his father-in-law had got five years' imprisonment for fraud.

I went to see his wife in the evening. She said that Allen wanted me to go to Phoenix with her and her daughter when the time was right. I told her that I didn't want to go, as I didn't like some of the people he was connected with such as Leslie Payne, who was once on the Kray firm - he had helped hold me the night Ronnie Kray burnt me with the pokers in Esmerelda's Barn.

On Friday I phoned the airport to see if my ticket to Paris was at the desk. I was told it was, and given my flight time and told I would be landing at Orly Airport. When I got there, I checked in my bags, and had a couple of hours to kill, so I had a nice meal and a few drinks.

The time passed quite quickly and we were told to go to the departure lounge. When we were called to board the plane I found out I was travelling first class.

By the time I had had a few drinks we were landing at Orly Airport. As I came out through customs I saw a chap holding up a board with my name on it. He said he had come to pick me up.

He took my bags, and put them in a silver Rolls Royce. As we were going along, he said to me that this was the car I would be driving while I was here. He seemed a nice bloke and his name was Jack Frager. He told me that he was Canadian and that he had been with Bob Gould since he was about 17 years old.

We were going along the Champs Elysées. It hadn't taken us that long to get there, and we then turned into a street called Rue de Pointou. We stopped outside number 25. He told me that this was their Paris office.

When we got to Bob's office, he was waiting for me. He

came over and shook my hand. He told me that Allen Cooper had been to see him the day before and that he had got a plane to the States. He asked me if I had any money. I told him all I had was English money. He said, "Don't worry," and gave me a bundle of French francs.

We had a couple of drinks and he already had some food laid on for me. He asked me about England, and said he was glad the Kray twins had got 30 years in prison. He thought they were both mad, and told me how Ronnie Kray had sliced off the right hand of a young friend of his with a machete knife one night in the West End. All the Kray brothers did was use people.

He told me I was not to worry; while I was working for him I would be well looked after. He then told Jack to take me to the hotel where they were staying.

We drove up to the Arc de Triomphe and into Boulevard Wagram and Jack pulled up outside a beautiful hotel. The hotel porter came out and carried my bags inside. I booked in at the desk and went by the lift to our floor. The bellboy opened my room door and put my bags inside.

Jack tipped him and helped me unpack my bags. Then we went down to the bar and had a few drinks together. Jack said he had to go and pick up Bob and bring him back to the hotel. I said I would go back to my room and have a bath and change. It was a beautiful room, with an en suite bathroom, and it was stocked up with drinks. After a couple of hours there was a knock on the door.

It was Jack. He said Bob was down in the bar waiting for

us. We had a few more drinks, then Bob said, "Let's go and have a meal." We went to a very select restaurant just outside Paris. The food was out of this world. All the staff in there knew Bob well and they couldn't do enough for us. He ordered champagne and brandy.

It was getting late and Bob paid the bill and tipped the waiters. I thought that they would never stop shaking my hand.

As we were on our way back to the hotel, Bob said he would give me a call in the morning. We had a few more drinks in the bar and then we went to our rooms. I put my head on the pillow and I was gone.

The next day, Jack drove me round Paris and showed me some of the well-known places. We finished up at Notre Dame. On our way back to the office he said, "Right, you can drive."

He was surprised at how good a driver I was and from then on I drove Bob's Rolls.

I had been in Paris for about two months when Bob told me to go to a large house just outside Paris and pick up two men as I would be driving them about all day.

When I arrived, I was shown through the large gates and up to a beautiful house. Two men came out carrying black bags. One got into the back. The other one sat next to me. He directed me where I should go.

I drove them round Paris all day and they went into all sorts of places. Finally, I dropped them off where I had picked them up and then went back to my hotel. I had a couple of drinks at the bar and then went to my room.

I had just got out of the bath when Bob came in. He said, "I'll be in the bar."

Bob got Jack and me a drink and said that he had ordered a car to drive us that evening, as he didn't like to drink and drive.

We had a chauffeur driven car take us to a restaurant just outside Paris. It was owned by two gay men, and when we were shown to our table, the two men who I had been driving around that day were already seated there. We all shook hands and sat down to our meal.

The food was out of this world. Bob ordered my main meal and when the waiter brought it to me, he put a large dinner plate in front of me and then served me with this large joint of meat. I looked at Bob and asked if he wanted me to carve the meat.

Bob burst out laughing. "No, Len, that's yours." It was a whole rib of beef.

We had a lovely evening and on the way home to our hotel Bob gave me 3,000 francs. He said that was for driving them about that day.

We got to the hotel and Bob went up to his room.

I asked Jack, "Who were those two men?"

Jack said they were the Paris collectors. I didn't ask anymore. I knew better.

A couple of days later, Jack and I went out for a meal in the evening. Bob was away on business.

Jack had his own silver shadow Rolls Royce, which Bob

had given him as a birthday present. As we went into the hotel we were suddenly surrounded by police. They handcuffed us, put us in a van, and drove us to their headquarters.

We were taken inside and he put Jack in a big wire cage. It was filled with pimps and prostitutes. There were no mattresses or blankets. I was put into a cell.

He spent three days in there with nothing but water and some dark bread. I couldn't speak French and they pretended they couldn't speak English.

On the fourth morning I was taken to an office where a man was sitting at a large desk. For the first few minutes we just looked at each other and then he spoke my name in English. I told him that I wanted to see the British Consul and I demanded to know why I had been arrested.

He asked if I was hungry.

I answered, "Are you taking the piss?" All I had been given was water and this stinking bread.

"I want to know why you have arrested me and Jack. We have done nothing wrong!"

He said that he knew all about me.

He had been in touch with Scotland Yard and they had told him that I had been on the Kray case. Then he said that Bob had been thrown out of England as an undesirable alien. I said that I didn't know anything about that. I again demanded to see someone from the British Embassy.

He picked up the phone and said something in French and two big plain-clothes cops came in. They put all my property on his desk and told me to pick it up. Then he told me that these two men would take me outside and I could buy whatever food I liked and also some cigarettes.

I came back with drinks, long French bread, sandwiches and two hundred cigarettes.

I was taken back to the nick and seated in a corridor. I gave food and fags to the other people there and they all started shaking my hands and kissing me on the cheeks.

Sometime later I was taken back to the office and was told Jack and I were free to go and a car would drive us to our hotel. They also apologised for any inconvenience that we had been put through.

So I said, "Before I go, could you tell me why we were arrested in the first place?"

All he would say was that we were arrested on suspicion. Jack knew France like the back of his hand and we were soon pulling up in front of a hotel in Chantilly. We had barely stopped when the hotel porters were outside ready to take our bags for us. I suppose it was the sight of seeing two Rolls Royces pull up outside.

We were quickly shown to our rooms. I had a nice shower and changed my clothes and went down to the bar. Bob was already in there with a friend, who came from Geneva, with his young lady. Sir Peter Moon was there also.

I liked Peter; he was a happy-go-lucky man who loved a drink and a gamble. Jack came down and told Bob everything that had happened in Paris. They all laughed when I told them Jack had been put in a big cage with all the pimps and prostitutes. We had supper; then I retired for the night.

The next morning I had my breakfast and went for a walk. It was a lovely day and it was nice to see some countryside again. I got back to the hotel around midday.

Bob gave me a coffee and said, "You're in luck, there's racing on today." The course was just across the road from the hotel.

I went to the races that afternoon. Wally Swinburn was riding there. I backed him but he didn't win. Still, I came out winning a few francs by the end of the day.

We left Chantilly on Monday and spent the next couple of months stopping at different places, like Marseille, Montpellier, Beziers, Narbone and finally Toulouse. We stayed in the Hotel Concord for about three weeks. We then drove to Madrid, and stayed there for a few months. While I was there I lived in a hotel near the palace in a street called Avenue St Antonio. I didn't like Madrid; it was very dusty and the police were all armed and looked most threatening, carrying long batons at their sides.

I used to go into old Madrid most evenings and drink in the Flamingo bars, but I was missing England so much. I missed having pie and mash and going to Tubby Isaac's stall in Aldgate to have my fill of jellied eels and other fish food. Most of all I was fed up of living out of a suitcase.

It was getting near Christmas. Bob said that they were going back to Paris as we had some business to clear up there. We arrived back in Paris about two weeks before Christmas and I stayed at the Ave Du Gallie Hotel off the Champs Elysées for a few days.

Bob took us out to dinner one evening and said he was going to spend Christmas in Majorca and that I could go anywhere in the world to spend Christmas.

Sir Peter Moon said that he was going home to England so I said to Bob that that was what I would like to do. Bob okayed that, and before I left, he gave me an address in London where a good friend of his lived, where I could pick up some money — you couldn't bring French francs out of the country. Bob said I was to meet Sir Peter at Heathrow airport two weeks after Christmas and he would see us in Paris.

I never did meet Sir Peter and that was the last I ever saw of any of that lot.

33

back to the krays again

I STAYED AT my sister Lil's for a while until I found myself somewhere to live.

I went into a pub called The Hayfield for a drink in the Mile End Road. Harry 'Jew Boy' was at the bar. He got me a drink and said that I looked well. I told him that I haven't been about for a few years. He was a smart arse and he had been very close to the Kray twins.

We had a couple of drinks, then all of a sudden he started to cry. He said to me, "Lenny, what do you think of my two boys?"

"Who?" I said.

"My Ronnie and Reggie. They've got to do 30 years. They will be old men when they come out."

"I do feel sorry for Reggie, but Ronnie was fucking mad.

Look what he did to me Harry, and for what? You don't like to see anyone do bird, but I am like a lot of people in the East End – I'm glad Ronnie is where he belongs."

"Lenny, you're right. Fuck them. They were wicked bastards, they have ruined and hurt a lot of people in the East End and if hanging was still the law, they would have been hanged."

Now here was a man who had been glad to be in their company before they got nicked and here was a man that used to drink with their father, and went into their mother's home.

I looked at him with disgust and said, "Blimey, you've soon changed your tune."

I put my drink down on the counter and walked out. I have never spoken to the bloke since.

I went into the 81 Club. They all asked me where I had been and we went next door to The Three Crowns to have a drink. The pub owner came over, kissed me, and wished me good luck. We all had a good drink and it was nice to see their smiling faces again.

The East End had changed; there was no more organised crime, and people could go into pubs with no fear. I don't think there will ever be anyone like the Kray twins again, thank God.

They may have ruled with fear, but in the end hardly anyone was loyal to them. I pity the poor people who were loyal to the end — what did they get out of it?

My old mate of many years, Bertie Hook, lives on the Isle

of Dogs and one of his neighbours is Ronnie Bender, Ronnie Kray's driver who was in the house in Evering Road when Reggie Kray butchered Jack the Hat to death. Ronnie was one of the firm who was ordered to clean the flat up and to help get the body out of there. He didn't really have any choice in the matter else he would have ended up like Jack the Hat. Ronnie was very loyal to the Krays. He kept his mouth shut and got a 20-year prison sentence of which he served 18 years.

Ronnie's dear wife, Buddy, had to bring her children up on her own. She had to scrimp and scrape to get the money to go and see her husband in prisons all over the country. With all the money the Krays have been allowed to earn while inside with their books and films, they have never given a single penny to Ronnie Bender or his wife. On top of that, Charlie Kray stopped people giving Ronnie Bender a benefit night when he came out of prison on Reggie Kray's orders.

He said that Ronnie Kray was in more need of the money because he was in debt in Broadmoor. That was all the thanks Ronnie and his wife got from the Krays for all those years of loyalty. There really is no honour among thieves.

Ronnie spent 18 years inside, Buddy spent 18 years outside, but despite all that they both went through, she waited for him and they are still together today. Buddy really deserves a medal.

I don't think Bender knew what was going to happen. He told me he was there because he loved Ron Kray. That's not something I can understand, but he did worship him. Ronnie remembers Ronnie Kray with affection and recalls how Ronnie used to give him clothes, but he could be forgetful. Once he gave Bender a lovely pair of crocodile shoes. Bender walked around in them for a few days and lapped up the appreciative comments. A couple of days later Bender went out for the night with Ronnie. They went to a club, had a few drinks and were getting on fine. But then suddenly Ronnie Kray stopped in his tracks and glared at Bender. Bender had no idea what he had done wrong. Then Ronnie switched to his most menacing expression and shouted, "What are you doing with my shoes on?"

So you can see once again that this is the way the Krays supposedly looked after their own. Organised crime has been busted now in the East End, and I hope that is the last we see of that scourge.

After the Krays were locked away, the police cracked down on anyone who showed the remotest signs of taking over the twins' old patch.

One police target were the Dixon brothers who were still young and handy, despite having been around for a few years. Alan and George Dixon were said to have been the main muscle for the firm run by Phil Jacobs, who owned The Plough and Harrow at Leytonstone.

In July 1972, Jacobs was sent down for twelve years and Alan for nine. Everyone thought the sentences were extremely harsh, but the authorities were taking no chances after taking so long to nail the Krays and the Richardson gang in South London.

I still see Alan Dixon around the East End these days. It doesn't matter where we meet — in a pub or in the street — he always kisses me on the lips. Very affectionate fellow is Alan. A bloody good man. I have known him since I did my spiels in the early sixties.

George and Alan used to mind Philly's pub for him. George was shot at once by Ronnie Kray in the Green Dragon Club in Aldgate. The gun failed to go off and Ronnie gave him the bullet. What a generous guy!

It was nonsense that they were going to take over from the Krays when they were put inside. The Dixons were never liberty takers and were nothing like the Krays. I never found anything wrong with George and Alan.

All you have now are drug-related crimes and people going about mugging the old. To me these muggers are the scum of the earth. And I think that I speak for all normal people when I say it makes you sick to the stomach to see all these poor helpless old men and women getting knocked senseless by these evil bastards.

People say to me, "Ain't you afraid of recounting all your dealings with the Krays?"

I don't feel afraid. I have only told the truth and what more can they do to me?

I am now 70 years old, and have had eight heart attacks. I suffer from severe vascular disease and I am in constant pain. I am registered disabled and each day I live is a bonus. I have a beautiful wife and I also have a beautiful daughter who is thirteen. I would not swap them for all the money in the world.

I have still got some good true friends and my best mate, Bertie Hook. All I want now is to spend whatever time I have left in peace.

As I have always said I was on the case against Ronnie Kray because he was the one who tortured me. I am not sorry that he is dead, and I know that a lot of other people are glad too, because he hurt so many people in the East End. He thought that he was a God and could get away with anything. Well, he thought wrong because some people had the guts to stand up to him and his cronies.

Not one of the firm came out of their dealings with the Krays with any money and some of them have done a lot of bird for their leaders. The only ones who have come out with money are the Krays. If Ronnie Bender had done 18 years in prison for keeping his mouth shut for genuine thieves, he and his wife would have been looked after, and looked after well. I went to prison in 1953 for a family of Wapping dockers because I kept my mouth shut. My wife was looked after while I was away and so was I when I came home. That's what you call genuine people, and I don't know any of the firm who has had any money from the Krays. The truth is that the only ones they have looked after are themselves.

They say that time is a good healer and people tend to forgive and forget. I don't think the people that the Krays hurt in their heyday will ever forget or forgive because no one in thier right mind likes to see any member of their family cut to pieces, shot or beaten senseless.

The East End has changed now. Gone are the days when

you only had a piece of string to open the front door. People have now got iron gates to protect their front doors and steel grills on the windows. Yes, the East End has changed. A lot of the old cockneys have either died or moved further away. The East End pubs have lost their atmosphere and it's not safe to walk the streets on your own anymore. I feel sorry for all these young kids that are growing up — what have they got to look forward to?

Many lies have been written about the Krays, but you can't only blame the Krays for this. If there had not been so many bent police about at the time, the Krays would not have got as big as they did. But that is the way of life — you will always have criminals and you will always have corrupt police. Wherever money is concerned, you will always find you have bad apples in all walks of life. Some policemen don't care that they have fitted you up as long as they get a conviction. Even today there are people locked up in prisons either put there by grasses or who have been fitted up by the bent police. But at the same time, where would we be if we didn't have the many honest police officers.

Eventually I stopped doing any more 'jobs' as it was getting too much; too many people were doing it. But in all my time as a thief I never touched any East End homes. If I had done so, I would never have been able to carry on living in my home district.

So much rubbish has been written and said over the years about how the East End streets were safer when the Krays were around, how they only hurt their own and were perfect gentlemen to woman and children. Some foolish people say that if the Krays had still been around there would be no muggings, and it would be safe for old folk to walk the streets without fear of attack. Well, that's absolute crap.

The East End has changed so dramatically along with the wider society. The Krays, even if they wanted to which they wouldn't, would not have been able to do anything about the type of crimes such as muggings which go on today.

They were powerful at a different time and symbolise that time. They would not have lasted very long in the present day. Different times bring forth different types of criminals and gangsters.

In their numerous books and pronouncements, the Krays seems to have played scant attention to the truth. A recent example is the revelations about the murder of Frank Mitchell, a notorious criminal who the Krays did admit to breaking out of jail and then hiding. Mitchell then disappeared, before they had him executed.

For 30 years, the Krays claimed they had nothing to do with the Frank Mitchell murder. However, Freddy Foreman has recently revealed that he killed Mitchell as a favour to the Krays. This, again, only goes to show what hypocrites the Krays really are.

I sometimes wonder if I did the right thing, by going on the Kray case. I went on it to protect my two children knowing full well what could have happened to them if the Krays ever got hold of me. To tell you the truth, I didn't care about myself, my first thoughts were for my children's safety.

But when the children grew up, they turned against me. They stopped speaking to me and even called me a grass. Believe me, that really hurts.

I still love my kids and always will but that's what thanks I got for putting my life on the line for them. I hope that one day they will know the truth and stop listening to people who don't know what they are talking about.

Yes, I went on the Kray case, I stood in the dock, and I would do it all again under the same circumstances. I have been called a grass for it. But I can honestly say that, each time I stood in the dock at different courts, I was always there on my own. I don't care what some people say I can hold my head up high. Yes, I have had nice clothes, I've been to different countries and I have had lots of things by being a thief. But I never once robbed my own. And yes, I have had to pay a big price for the way I chose to live my life.

The people that I think suffered the most out of the Kray business are my friends, Ronnie Bender and his wife. He has been called a Judas by the Krays. All through the years the Kray twins have kidded people that they were good men. But it is mostly folk who didn't know them, or weren't even born when the Krays were put away, who believe them.

Well, everybody has a right to their own opinion. The press has helped glamorise the Krays over the years and all the books they have written and videos and the T-shirts have really given the public the wrong impression of the Krays. But the East Enders knew what they were really like.

The Krays killed George Cornell and said he was a petty

crook. Well, I knew George well, and I would always have backed him against them in a one-to-one fight.

Jack the Hat was another victim who they have tried to put down by calling him a petty thief Again I knew Jack, and I know that he was a good money-getter. Sadly, neither George nor Jack are here to defend themselves. But people who knew them know the truth.

Doesn't it seem strange how the Krays were so ready to blacken people's names? Well, what about them? While I was on the Kray case a high-ranking police officer said to me he always thought people from the East End were a bit cute, meaning clever. So I asked him what he meant.

He told me that some of the police officers that were on the Krays' payroll were getting higher rankings due to the bodies the Krays were giving them. I was shocked at the time. But this went on while the Krays were at liberty.

After all those years in prison, none of the Krays showed any remorse for their crimes. I am not frightened by them anymore. If this book causes someone to hurt me, the one thing the Krays can't take away from me is the fact that I have spoken out for myself and for some of the men and the families they have hurt, whose lives they have ruined: George Cornell's daughter, who never knew her father; Jack 'The Hat' McVitie's wife; Frank Mitchell's family; the barmaid who witnessed Ronnie Kray shoot George Cornell in the Blind Beggar; Blonde Carol, whose house the Krays commandeered when Reggie butchered Jack; Ronnie Bender who lost 18 years of his life; Chrissy Lambrianou who lost 15 years of his life; Terry who I saw getting slashed to pieces and had to have 137 stitches; and poor old Billy Exley who was tormented by them, and who I am sad to say has since passed away.

Association with the Krays has even brought down people in high society. Some have had to give up their homes and move to other parts of the country, some going abroad.

I love the East End and I made up my mind that the Krays were not going to make me move from the place I have lived all my life. I am too old and too sick now to leave.

But one thing I can thank God for is that I have the most wonderful woman in my life. She is worth her weight in gold and I have a beautiful daughter who has made my life complete. When I look back over the years, whoever would have thought that a little street urchin like me from the back streets of the East End could have had so much money go through his hands? I have had plenty but people who know me know that I have given plenty away. That is what is meant by helping your own .

Any time that the Krays have done something for charity, they have always made it their business to advertise it so that they could make themselves look good, trying to kid people that they are not really bad people. East End people who really knew them, knew what they were really like. As I have always said, you can kid some of the people some of the time, but not all of the people all the time.

I know that the East End is a far better place without them. This country has never seen two gangsters like the twins and I hope that there will never be anybody like them again. I honestly think that the way they killed people shows that they are both completely mad to have committed such terrible crimes.

After all, the victims were human beings with families. The Krays can't blame anyone but themselves for being locked up because most of their own firm turned against them in the end. But you can't blame them, because when Nipper Read nicked the Krays, all they were thinking of was themselves and how they could get away with it.

That's why Ronnie Bender's sister got him his own lawyer. Because of that the Krays slagged him off, just like they have done to a lot of people who didn't do things the way they wanted them done.

Can't some of these Kray followers see what it would have been like today if they have never been arrested in 1968, and they had continued to operate and terrorise the East End? They would have been involved in all the same rackets. They didn't care how they got their money, just so long as it kept on flowing in.

If they had got away with the murders, there's no telling how many more people would have been sliced up and killed. They would have become even stronger and the police would have been frightened to nick them. I think they would have become untouchable. Even people in high places seemed to be wary of them.

In Ronnie Kray's autobiography, *My Story*, he proved yet again what a liar he was, trying to fool people into believing he was really a nice chap. I never did any business with the Krays as he tried to make out, as I knew that if you did anything for them you were lucky if you actually got paid.

In the prologue of his book he writes about a man called Billy Blake, but he was really writing about me.

According to Ronnie Kray, Billy Blake disfigured Buller Ward's son and Buller went to the police. They didn't want to know. This is the first lie, as some one like Buller Ward would never go to the police. He would always try to settle things for himself.

Ronnie wrote that he grabbed Billy Blake around the throat and told his victim he should never hurt women, children or old people. But it wasn't Ronnie who grabbed me around the throat. It was a couple of his firm's henchmen. And as for the warning about women, kids and the elderly, he should have been saying those things to himself.

He was the one who hated women. We know Ronnie liked young boys and the only people the Krays looked after were themselves. He claimed they earned millions, but not one of their firm came away with any money.

He said they paid a high price for the way they led their lives, and I can reply quite rightly, they deserved it. They ruined a lot of lives.

In his book, Ronnie Kray also writes of a straight man that came to see him because a chap from Mile End had broken his daughter's nose in three places. He gets very confused in his storytelling because he then claimed that I was the man from Mile End. As Ronnie tells it, the police did not want to know so he, the great benevolent godfather, intervened. He summoned the man from Mile End to Esmerelda's Barn and dished out justice by burning him with pokers. What a load of rubbish! He hoped that the man from the East End still bears the scars from the attack.

Well I'm sorry to disappoint him, but I had my face treated and there are no visible scars. The only scars left are under the skin.

It makes me sick to see how they tried to make themselves out to be such good fellows. They seemed to think the East End would not survive without them to lord over the manor. Well, it has been a much better place without them.

We still have crime, but then, short of Utopia, you will always have crime. But we don't have the type of crime that the Krays ran — the protection rackets and all the heartache they brought to a lot of people, both rich and poor. They thought they were gods. But there is only one God and he made the Krays pay for all the terror they wrought.

34

blowing
the safe

I HOPE THAT I have been at pains to point out that I have been no angel throughout my life. That doesn't mean to say that things weren't very funny at times!

Early in the 1960s, I was once in the 81 Club in Mile End Road. A chap who I knew quite well asked me to drive him in his car to see someone. I agreed. He got out of the car and went to see this chap in his factory. While I was sitting outside I looked around and saw two tin gates. As the wind whipped a bit they were making quite a loud cracking noise. About five minutes later my mate jumped in the car and said, "Quick, have it away."

"What's up?" I asked

"I have had to shoot the bastard," he said.

I drove him back to the 81 Club. I know that he is still alive today and if he reads this he will know who I am writing about. He is still a good mate of mine. We went on a few safe-blowing jobs together.

Once I was with a small team and we were off to blow a safe in the City of London. The man who was going to blow the safe had to go to the other side of London to get the jelly and detonators. We waited for him for four hours until 4.30 p.m. One of the firm that struck the job up started getting restless because me and a mate of mine had to go into the premises before they were locked up, so we could later let our accomplices in. So they phoned another chap, who they said could blow a safe as he had all the right equipment to do the job and arranged to meet him outside Aldgate Street Station.

Once that was done, we had a reserve in case the first choice did not arrive. So me and a bloke I'll call Sam went to the premises and hid in the boiler room. They closed the building at six o'clock in the evening, but to make sure everybody had finished for the day we waited until half past six.

All was secure and we set about turning the alarms off. Once we had done that, we opened the front doors up. We gave the signal and the rest of the team came in. I asked them where Bill was. He was the man who went to get the gear in the first place. They said he had still not returned. So they brought a bloke called Ken in to blow the safe. He was a big stocky chap who I knew quite well. Once we were all inside I said to Ken, "Are you sure you know what you're doing?" He replied, "Don't worry, it's a piece of cake."

I had my doubts about him, but I thought, Who am I to criticise? So we made our way to the third floor where the wages office was. The safe was a Chattsworth Millner. Ken started packing the jelly into the keyhole. I'd been on a few safe jobs and when I saw how much jelly he was forcing into the safe I asked him again, "Are you sure you know what you're doing?"

He replied with total confidence, "Leave it to me."

By now we had cut up quite a bit of carpet to put over the safe to muffle the noise when the safe blew. Ken said it was all ready. We covered the safe with the carpet and Ken ran the wire that was connected to the detonator to the battery that was going to set it off.

"Right," Ken said, "Everybody ready?"

He touched the wire to the battery. There was an enormous bang. Ken had blown the safe out of the window. The safe door went whizzing past us. All the money was blown to pieces and most of the ceiling came down. Pieces of money were floating by like confetti at a wedding.

We looked at each other in amazement. When the shock began to wear off I said, "Well, one thing's for sure. Ken's done a good job. He's cut the money up for us."

Once we had all got out safe and sound we headed for the pub.

We sat down and everybody burst out laughing. Everybody was in stitches. But one thing was for sure – we never used Ken on any more safe jobs.

35

those
krays again

THAT EXPERIENCE was one of the reasons I went to work on my own; I had only myself to worry about. If I kept my mouth shut, there was nobody to grass on me. I can't tell you about the jobs I did on my own as I could still get nicked for them.

It was true what Ronnie Kray said in his book about the smell of my burning flesh when he put the pokers on my face. I was told by a specialist that while Ronnie Kray was torturing me it made him come his lot — that's how he got his pleasure. I have always been one to live and let live, and even when I gave my evidence against Ronnie Kray, in my heart I didn't feel right about it. But I knew whatever people thought about me, I had to put the children first and if by chance I lose my life by writing this, I know that I did the right thing.

The swinging 60s were the right words for it because they were the best years of my life. I think that the music then was the best we will ever hear. It was in the early 60s that I met a man called Jacky Van Dongen, who came out of Wapping. He invited me to a party one Friday night in Hackney. It was held in a basement flat. The owner was a German, and it became our regular Friday night party. It was somewhere we would all meet up. He was a nice chap and I nicknamed him — unsurprisingly — Herman the German. Everybody enjoyed themselves and there was never any trouble.

One night we were all invited to a party in Grosvenor Buildings near the Blackwall Tunnel. The buildings were well over a century old and have long since been demolished. It was while we were at this party that a young lady got out of a taxi holding some bags, a fold-up pram and a young kid. As the flats had no lifts, I went down to give her a hand. By the time we had got to her flat on the fourth floor, I was knackered. She left the door open for me to go in with her bags. She was a very good-looking girl and it was no surprise to me when she told me that she worked in a nightclub as a hostess.

When I looked at the little boy I realised he was the spitting image of Reggie Kray. She noticed me looking at the child and asked me if I knew Reggie.

I said, "I have never heard of him."   .

She thanked me for helping her and I told her I was going back to the party. As I got to the door she thanked me again and that's when she said to me, "You are right. He is Reggie Kray's son."

She told me that she was terrified of the gangland boss and that if he found me in her flat there would be murders. She made me promise that I would not say anything to anyone about it when I returned to the party. I respected her wishes, and until now I have never said a word to anyone. I would like to think that the woman and her son have had a happy and peaceful life.

I never thought of writing a book about my dealings with the Krays until their own books turned into a torrent of self-justification and self-congratulation. I got so fed up with them slagging me off and also a lot of good people, trying to make themselves look like angels.

Tony Lambrianou said Reggie had done nearly 30 years and had never complained. Well, what have they got to complain about? I think they should think themselves lucky that hanging had been abolished in this country when they were convicted of murder.

I don't understand how Tony Lambrianou keeps standing by them. If you read Ronnie Kray's book, he calls Tony a grass, then states that at the time Reggie killed Jack 'The Hat', Tony wasn't even on the firm. That's the thanks he got for doing 15 years in the nick for them.

I am pleased Tony Lambrianou got himself a few bob for his books. After all, there have been plenty since the Krays were put away.

Look what the Krays have got away with in prison.

Charlie Kray spent the rest of his life in prison following a conviction on drug charges. He was supposed to be the quiet one. All the big money in crime these days is drug related. I call it blood money — I see all these young kids getting hooked on drugs, and some of them pay for it with their lives. It has ruined a lot of families. Even the poor old people getting mugged and badly beaten for a few pence are often victims of drugs, as their attackers will do anything for the money to pay for their next fix.

So many times I have heard the claptrap that there would be no muggings if there were people like the Krays around the East End. Well you only need to look at Charlie Kray to see this would not be the case. A lot of the muggings are drug related.

Some people say it's a shame that Charlie was sent down as he was an old man. Well I say, if he was guilty, as he was found, they should throw away the key. Some young kids will never have the chance to grow old because of drugs.

Barbara Windsor once had an affair with Charlie Kray. She still maintains what nice fellows they all were. Doesn't she realise that they only used her to boost their prestige? They were out-and-out gangsters and having their photographs taken with film stars and members of the aristocracy was just a way of building their egos.

I'll tell you, one word out of place from any of them and they would have seen the real Krays. If they had caught Ronnie on a bad day, the lot of them would have shit

303

themselves. I think a lot of them are hypocrites, running with the pack when it suits them.

Ronnie Kray was a homosexual, who hated women but loved young boys. The only woman that Ronnie loved was his mother. I was once in a drinking club in Rathbone Place off Oxford Street, and at the bar was a beautiful girl, who could have been no more than 25 years old. She was standing there with this man having a quiet drink. It was early evening and suddenly the door burst open and there, at the foot of the stairs, stood Ronnie Kray and about a dozen of his cronies. They went straight up to the man and knocked him down, and then they gave him a right good kicking. She was screaming and calling Ronnie Kray all sorts of names. Then he cut her down the side of her face, calling her a slag and flounced off.

Me and my mate couldn't get out of there fast enough. On the way back to the East End we made a pact never to say anything about this attack. Otherwise the heat would have been on us. Some time later I heard that the girl Ronnie cut that night had an old man who was in prison, and the chap she was having a drink with that night was, in fact, her brother. So just where do people get the idea from that they never hurt women?

I know for a fact that they would hurt anyone who got in their way. I suppose that they must have paid the woman and her brother to keep their mouths shut, since we never heard anything about that particular attack again.

I must admit I have always admired a good thief. Ones

who got out and did a good job and never hurt anyone while carrying out their business.

Someone told me years ago that thieves and villains never mix and the reason why is that there are so many grasses out there willing to put you away for a few quid. I have always said the bigger the chain, the weaker the link, meaning the more people involved in a crime the more chance you have got of getting nicked, since you will invariably get someone boasting about the job.

The ones I can't tolerate are those dirty bastards who go about robbing the poor old people incapable of defending themselves. I hate those bastards more than I hate the Krays. Even today people are having to live like prisoners in their own homes.

I saw pubs in the East End empty within minutes when the Krays and some of their firm walked in. People were scared to speak in their presence, let alone look at the twins. One word out of place or the odd glance towards them could have set it all off and someone could end up getting badly hurt.

Most of the people in the East End knew the real Krays and what they were all about. Even today, nearly 30 years later, most people would say that the Krays were wicked bastards and deserve everything they got.

They set out to terrorise people, they maimed people, and they ran their fake firms and protection rackets. They finally reached their ultimate goal, which was murder.

I believe that when Ronnie Kray walked into the Blind

Beggar pub in Whitechapel Road on that fateful evening and shot George Cornell at point blank range it was the start of their downfall. When Reggie Kray carved Jack the Hat up at Blonde Carol's and left his lifeless body on the floor in a pool of blood, it was just a matter of time before the twins would be arrested and get the punishment they so rightly deserved. They have always blamed other people for getting into bother, but they knew what they were getting into and for that they have had to pay the price, and quite rightly so.

Years ago when I used to work at Billingsgate Fish Market, the fish porters used to shout out "Up the hill!" and you would see some down-and-outs get behind their barrows loaded down with fish and give them a push up the hill. For that they would get a few pence. I have seen George Cornell get a few of these down-and-outs and give them some money so they could get themselves something to eat. He was like a king to them and they had a lot of respect for him. He was always willing to help people down on their luck.

Jack McVitie died because money meant nothing to him. It was gone as fast as he got it. I'll give you one instance. I had to meet him in a pub in the East End one day in the days when the pubs were split into different bars. Jack had just had a good tickle and, as he was about to leave, he went over to a table where some old people were sitting with their glasses of stout, mild and Guinness. He put his hand in his pocket, took out a wad of cash and put it on the table, saying to them, "'Ere, that'll keep you all in drink for a while."

With that he just turned and walked out of the pub. And the Krays have the cheek to call him no good. I will leave that to your own judgement.

Yes, the Krays did love their mother but so do millions of other people. I for one liked Violet Kray, she was a very fine lady, but you can't tell me that she did not know what was going on and what the twins were up to. She must have been suspicious when George Cornell's widow went to her home and threw bricks through her windows .

In the sixties there was a spieler in Campbell Road, Bow, which was owned by an Asian man whose name was Ali. About 11 a.m. one day, me and a couple of others were standing in the club talking when suddenly the door opened and in walked a man, about five feet tall. He wore a Sinatra-style trilby and slung over his shoulders was a very expensive mohair overcoat. He called over to Lou, who was behind the bar, and asked him if Ali was in.

Lou told the little chap that Ali wasn't in and he had no idea when he would be back.

The little man reacted instantly. He pulled out a gun and fired two shots into the ceiling. Then he shouted out, "Tell Ali that Fast Cars has been to see him."

He calmly walked out of the club and down the alley. We went to see where he went next. He got into a big green American car and as he pulled away you could just about see his head over the seat.

We went back into the club and asked Lou, "Who was that chap?"

He replied, "How do I know who fucking Fast Cars is?"

He then told us he was going to lock the club up and since that day I have never seen or heard of Ali again. The club is now a mosque.

They say it takes all sorts to make a world. Well, I think there is nothing further from the truth. How can some people think that the Krays were two nice misunderstood boys? Nothing is further from the truth. I think their so-called fan club should be looked into as some of them can't be all the ticket.

I was once in prison during the 1960s with a man from the East End. He was inside for nicking a lorry load of snout. He had a couple of marks down his face. He wasn't a villain, just a thief. He was doing five years because some bastard grassed him up. I was quite friendly with him. One day he said to me, "Len, I suppose you're wondering how I got these two scars on my face?"

I replied, "It's none of my business."

But he started to tell me anyway. Before he got his prison sentence he was taking a girl out and they had a row. It was all over between them. One day he walked into a pub and saw his old flame standing at a bar with a couple of her mates. As he got to the bar he said hello to all of them and bought them a drink. He was a good-looking chap. One of the friends of his ex said she fancied him. Not long after that Reggie Kray walked into the pub with some of the firm. He sent the girls and the man a drink. After a short while the man's ex started talking to Reggie Kray. When the man went to the toilet to take a leak, the toilet door opened and in came Reggie Kray. He told the man not to have a go at the girl. Reggie then pulled out a razor and cut the man twice across the face. Then Reggie punched the living daylights out of him. Later the man discovered that Reggie had taken his ex out a few times.

The poor bloke was just a thief, and he wouldn't hurt a fly. The Krays would hurt anyone when it suited them. This obviously created fear and terror in the East End. I have seen people politely say hello to the twins when they met them, but as soon as the Krays were out of earshot they would call them a right pair of liberty-takers.

That's how they reigned for so long — everyone in the East End was terrified of them.

A man called Teddy Passmore lived in Stepney. I have known him all my life. He was a nice hard-working bloke, who lost an eye when a man who lived in the street fired an arrow into the air and just as Ted looked up, the arrow came straight down and went right through his eye.

The chap who fired the arrow ended up on the Kray firm.

A few years later Teddy was paid for a claim of about eight thousand quid. In those days, that was quite a bit of money. One day Teddy asked me if I knew the Kray twins, but in those days I had no dealings with them. He told me that the twins had heard through someone that he had got paid out on a claim and he was so frightened of them that he had given them two grand. This was a man who wasn't a thief or a villain, but it was fear that made him pay up.

I'm very sorry to say that Ted has since passed away. But this little story just shows people what the Krays were really like. No one was safe with them out on the streets. I believe even their brother Charlie was frightened of them at times. I honestly believe that if it wasn't for them Charlie would have had a completely different kind of life and probably a much happier one.

I believe the twins should have written another book called The Lives We Have Wrecked.

The Regency Club in Hackney was owned by the Barry brothers, who were nice people, always willing to help someone out. I think it was the best drinking club in the East End, but like everything else, the Krays got their paws into it. They may have stopped some trouble, but they also caused a lot of it.

The Krays never looked after the firm members. I once got nine months and I knew the person I went away for. He was the same size as me and had black curly hair like me. While I was on remand I went to see this man who had actually done the job. I told him not to worry; that he was safe with me and I would take my chances. Unfortunately for me, it didn't do me any favours. When the man came to see me on a visit he brought his tailor along. He took my measurements and there were a couple of suits ready for me when I was released from prison.

It was during this stretch in Pentonville in B Block that we had some late arrivals come in one night. When our cells were opened in the morning to slop out, one of the new arrivals came up to me. He was a bit posh and he told me that he had never been in prison. He was doing 28 days for a fine. I showed him what to do and then he said he didn't like the soap he had been given to wash with. He asked me what the little pot of powder was for. I told him that it was to clean his teeth. He said he couldn't clean his teeth with this filthy stuff. I've found a right one here, I thought.

When I looked across the landing I noticed that the screw that was on duty that morning to take any applications from the cons was the most miserable bastard you could ever come across. That particular morning he had a face on him like a pig. That was actually what the cons called him.

So I asked this new con, who was beginning to drive me mad, which soap and toothpaste he had used on the outside. He told me. Then I said, "Not to worry. See that screw over there. You go and tell him what you want and he will make sure you get it sometime today."

Well, he went on his way over to The Pig and I said to a couple of the other cons to expect a good laugh. The con began talking to him when suddenly he went berserk and we could hear him shouting out to the con, "Where do you fucking well think you are? In some hotel? And if it's not too much to ask – what type of after-shave would you wish me to get you? Now fuck off, you horrible little bastard and don't come wasting my time or I will see to it that you are taken down the block."

Despite this incident I became good friends with the new arrival.

Another time when I was doing time in Pentonville the screws used to open three cells at a time to let us slop out in the morning. While we were doing this, we were not allowed to talk to the other cons. If you did and got caught, you were put on report.

There was one screw that we used to call Speedy, as he was so fast opening and banging you up. He was the only screw on our landing; on the other landings you had two screws doing the same job. He would have us all slopped out and banged up long before the screws on the other landings had finished. He was a slimy bastard always looking for some excuse to nick one of the cons. Then one morning as he was opening the cells we heard a racket. We could hear other screws running along the landing, and we could hear Speedy screaming. Whenever there was any trouble about a dozen screws always came at you. That's how brave they were.

When we opened up to go and get our breakfast we found out that Speedy had had a go at one of the cons when he opened his cell. The con threw a piss-pot all over him and Speedy was covered in piss and shit. The con that did it to Speedy was known as the Duchess because he was gay. We found out afterwards that when Speedy was on nights he used to open up another gay's cell late at night and try to have sex with him. But the man, called Bubbles, wasn't having any of it. So finally Speedy had forced Bubbles to give him a hand-job. Bubbles was a good-looking bloke; he had fair curly hair and the face of an angel. We had a few gays in our wing at the time and late at night you could hear the screws opening their cells and going in to have sex with them. For that the screws used to give them half an ounce of tobacco.

Some of the older screws were all right. It was the younger ones who were the bastards — they used to have hats pulled over their faces to resemble a guard in the army. We used to call them little Hitlers and low-lifes — how can any man lock up another like an animal?

I was a landing cleaner on the ones at the time when they brought a con up from the punishment block as we called it. He was in a right state and as soon as they banged him up in his cell he started smashing it up. About a dozen screws came to his cell, and looked through the spyhole to see where the con was. Then they got in as fast as they could, put him in a straight jacket and took him over to the hospital.

I was told to clean the cell up. As I was doing this a screw came in and said the bastard never got his own way. He wanted the screws to beat him up but they found out he was a masochist and enjoyed having pain inflicted on himself.

On another occasion the screw was late opening up one morning. He was a big ginger bastard and had a chip on his shoulder. He wore his hat like a guardsman and nobody liked him.

I had slopped out and was one of the last to get my razor blade. I had just shaved one half of my face when he was back to collect my blade because that is what you had to do each morning — hand back your blade. The other cons were on their way to breakfast. I told the screw I had not finished yet. But he still wanted me to give it to him. I told him he had been late opening that morning. He came into my cell and I knew right away what was going to happen. So before he could lay a hand on me I kicked him right in the bollocks and as he went down, I poured my washing water over him. He called me all the names under the sun as he went out banging the door shut. I knew what would happen next. I heard the screws' footsteps running towards my Peter.

By now all the other cons had had their breakfast. The keys in the lock turned and the door flew open. In they came, the brave bastards — all eight of them. I had no chance. The ginger one gave me a few slaps and then they dragged me out feet first along the landing. I managed to cup my hands behind my head and as they pulled me down the iron stairs my hands were taking the full impact. I was taken straight down to the chokey block and slung in a cell. They gave me a few more slaps before finally closing the door. I lay there with all the skin gone from the back of my hands. I had a couple of lovely bumps on my head. My nose and right eye were bleeding. I just lay there. The pain in my back was so intense I thought they had broken it. After a short time the cell door opened and one of the orderlies from the hospital came in. He examined me and verified that I had no broken bones. While he was cleaning me, he gave me a fag. He stopped the bleeding and bandaged up my hands. He gave me a couple of painkillers and as he went out, he looked back and said, "I'll see you later."

"Don't worry, I'm not going anywhere," I replied.

He smiled and closed the door. When he had gone, I thought, Well they're not all animals, after all. I heard the orderly speaking to the screw who was in charge of the chokey block. He said to him that this kind of brutality had got to stop. It was getting out of hand.

The cell was bare so I sat in the corner on the stone floor. A short while later the cell was unlocked and four screws came into the cell, including the ginger screw. He said to me that I was going on the Governor's report and if I told him that I had fallen down the stairs, they would go easy on me when I went in front of the Governor. What the hell, I thought, I can't beat them. I didn't look so bad now that I had been cleaned up, so I said, "OK."

Their attitude had changed towards me and they took me to see the Governor. Once you are in his office you have a screw standing on either side of you and then the complaining officer reads out the charge. After that was done, the Governor asked me how I had got in such a state. I told him that I fell down the stairs on my way to the chokey block. He asked me if I had anything further to add and I said no. He then said to me, "Do you know that you are on a serious charge and it is one that I can put you on a visiting committee for? However, after what I have been told by the officer concerned I will deal with your case

315

myself. You will do 14 days bread and water, loss of wages and loss of privileges." I was taken out of my cell to the chokey block where I would do my punishment.

It is quite understandable that the crime rate is going up. The East End will never be the same again because all the character has gone. The pubs are not the same; many are closing down. Gone are the days when your neighbours used to chat to one another over the back yards, or sit outside their street doors in the summer till late in the evening watching their children play happily in the streets. Even the little grocery shops and butchers are slowly disappearing. In those shops, the woman could have the goods put on tick till the end of the week.

The cinemas are closed down. Most of all, it's not safe to let the kids play in the streets. Yes, the old East End has changed. But, as I sit here with my mind going back over the years when all my family was alive and remembering all the things that have gone on in my life, I wouldn't want it any other way. I have three wonderful children and a wife in a million. What more could a man want.

My heart goes out to the many people who have suffered at the hands of the Kray twins over the years. I feel sorry for the people whose lives have been ruined by the twins. Only people who really knew the Krays realise what a pair of evil bastards they really were. They wanted respect but they never got it because to command respect, you have to show respect. People never respected the Kray twins; they were terrified of them.

The person I honestly felt sorry for is the twins' elder brother, Charlie. I knew him for more than 50 years, and always found him to be polite. I never heard him raise his voice to anyone and I think I am quite right in saying that if it hadn't been for the twins he wouldn't have gone to prison.

I once appeared on a television programme called *London Today* with the actress Helen Keating. I found her to be a pleasant person. When we had finished recording the programme, we had coffees in a small hospitality room. During our chat, Helen said that the twins' cousin, Ronnie Harts, was a grass and also that my dear old friend Ronnie Bender was one too.

When she said that I went cold; I was shocked. I asked her why she thought this and Helen told me she knew this to be true because Reggie Kray had said so.

It took me a few minutes to compose myself.

Then I turned to her and said, "Look, Helen, you are talking about a man, Ronnie Bender, who stayed loyal to the Kray twins, kept his mouth shut and for that he received a 20-year prison sentence, of which he served 18 years. His children were only kids when he went away and now they are grown men. The Krays never gave Ronnie or his wife and children one single penny for all the heartaches they went through because of Ronnie's steadfast loyalty to the Krays. Can you imagine all the grief that Ronnie's family has gone through during all those years?

She replied, "Well, I didn't really know him."

I told her not to be taken in by what Reggie Kray told her. He was using her like he did a lot of other people who visited him in prison. I told her that was his only way of getting his messages out of the nick. I also told her he was as cunning as a fox. I said that I was sorry for all the people he was using.

As for Reggie's wife, Roberta, she only met him when she went on a visit. She must have been about eight years old when he went away. I don't know her, but I have seen her on television, and to me she seems to be a nice person, someone you wouldn't associate with the Krays. Or maybe she is another one who wants to be in the limelight. No one had heard of her until she married Reggie Kray.

Reggie Kray once said that his life ended when the Hoxton girl he married, Frances Shea, died. I met Frances the first time in Amhurst Road, Hackney. The Krays had a big electrical shop on the corner. It was one of their many long-term frauds. Just around the corner Reggie was having a shop done out for her to sell records.

I was with a mate, Harry Abrahams, and Harry said to me then that Reggie had done himself a great favour because Frances was so beautiful and very smart.

Sometime later I saw her in Ridley Road Market in Dalston. I had to look two or three times before I recognised her. I said, "Hello."

She looked at me as if she was miles away.

I asked her, "When are you going to open your record shop?"

She replied, "Please don't talk to me because I am being followed and I don't want you to get into any trouble."

I looked around and saw that Frances was right, she was being followed. So I left her and slipped into the crowd.

That was the last time I ever saw her. She looked haggard and drawn. I could not believe my eyes. It wasn't until a few weeks later that I met an old mate of mine who had been with the Krays for a long time. His name was Billy Exley. He had gone on a job with me years ago and someone had grassed us up. When we had got to our destination I sussed that something was not right and I told Billy to get away. As we were doing this, we could see a load of Old Bill coming towards us. So Billy and I ran across some fields. We didn't know the area, and we came to a thicket. We both dived through it and found ourselves plunging twenty feet into a river. I helped Billy to the other side and finally we got to a phone box where I phoned a mate of mine and told him roughly where we were. It took him a few hours but he finally found us and got us back to the East End. Billy never forgot me for that.

I told Billy that I had seen Frances in Ridley Road Market and how terrible I thought she had looked. We were in a pub in Brick Lane at the time, having a drink. He liked to get away from them. He told me how sorry he felt for Frances.

Frances Shea had been a beautiful looking girl, who fell in love with Reggie Kray. Mr and Mrs Shea were dead against their daughter going out with him. They knew the type of person he really was, and if only Frances had listened to her parents who were very well respected by the people in the East End, she would have been alive today.

She was a very smart, good-looking girl, who could have had her pick of any man she wanted, but like many people Reggie Kray had manipulated, she was no exception. So finally, he got her to thinking his way, and she finally consented to marry him.

If only she had known what she was getting herself into. I know that Ronnie Kray was so paranoid against her, because in his sick mind he hated Frances, he didn't look upon her as his beautiful sister-in-law. No, quite the opposite. He looked upon her as an intruder, who had taken his other half, Reggie, away from him. I know that from the beginning of married life to Reggie, Frances was very happy being Mrs Reggie Kray. She was so often taken out to the West End, where she would wine and dine with numerous celebrities, who were so-called friends of the Kray twins.

Frances had never experienced this type of roller coaster life before, and with all the attention that was being bestowed upon her, it was enough to turn any young girl's head. Frances told me personally that she was fed up with the life she was leading, and all she wanted was what Reggie had told her, that they would live in the country and have a family. So as time went by, she finally realised that it was all false promises. Her days of wining and dining were slowly coming to an end. Reggie was now seeing more of Ronnie than he was of her, and Ronnie was pleased that he was getting his own way with Reggie. Poor Frances was slowly becoming a grass widow, being left on her own more. Well not quite on her own. There was always one or two of the firm left with her to keep her company. In effect, she was a prisoner in her own home.

As time went by, the life that she had to endure was putting her in a depressive state. So her only way out of this troubled life was to finally ask Reggie for a divorce. Reggie would not hear of this as nobody walks away from the Krays. When Reggie told Ronnie that Frances wanted a divorce, Ronnie's reply to Reggie was, "You can't let her have a divorce because she knows too much about our business." From that day, she was locked in the bedroom while the twins went up west to one of the many night clubs that they would frequent, returning home in the early hours of the morning. The line of treatment she was being subjected to was inhuman and very cruel. This type of cruelty that they put Frances through would make anyone's mind snap.

The final showdown came for Frances at about six o'clock one morning. Reggie and Ronnie returned to their flat in the early hours where they had left poor Billy Exley behind to make sure that Frances didn't get out of the bedroom and leave the flat. Billy was a very nice man and a very good friend of mine, but he was only one of the many who had to abide by their rules. Billy asked if he could go home now and the Colonel as Ronnie was called, told Billy to get his head down on the settee, as they might need him in the morning.

Ronnie and his young man retired to Ronnie's bedroom

while Reggie, together with his hostess, retired to his bedroom where Frances was lying in the bed, out cold from the sleeping tablets they had made her take before they went up west. Frances woke up in the morning, unaware of what had been going on in her own bed, horrified at what she was witnessing.

Reggie, her dear husband who wanted everybody to know how much he loved his dear wife Frances, was lying in the same bed with the hostess next to him. Frances tried to get out of the bedroom but Reggie had locked it from the inside when he came home and had hidden the key. The twins' minder who was on the other side of the door could hear Frances screaming and banging on the door, but alas poor Billy could do nothing about it. Who in their right mind would go against the Kray twins? Finally the bedroom door was opened and Frances came screaming out of the bedroom. Reggie followed her and gave her a couple of slaps about her face to try and calm her down. By now the hostess had got herself dressed and made a quick exit from the flat. Frances went back into the bedroom and got herself dressed. She came out still screaming at Reggie, asking what had she done to deserve that and calling Reggie a pervert.

Poor Billy Exley was standing there, not knowing what to do. By now Ronnie was awakened by the noise and as he entered the living room he started shouting at Reggie, "What the fucking hell is going on?" Before Reggie could give an answer, Frances made a dash for the street door. Ronnie Kray was right behind her, dragging her back into the living room by her hair. Ronnie and Reggie were shouting at one an other, as they finally got Frances back into the bedroom. Billy could hear Ronnie shouting at Reggie saying, "Stuff some fucking pills down her throat, that will shut the bitch up."

About half an hour had gone by and then the twins appeared out of the bedroom perspiring profusely. Ronnie was the first to speak saying, "That will keep the slag quiet for a while." Billy was ordered to pour out a drink for them and have one for himself. Ronnie collapsed into the armchair chain smoking, and the two of them were knocking back the gin as if it was going out of fashion.

As the drink was getting the better of them. Ronnie started shouting at Reggie, "I told you right from the start that no good would come of your marriage, but you wouldn't listen to me".

When the two of them had quietened down Billy said to Reggie. "I've got to go now as my wife will wonder where I've got to." Ronnie started going into a rage again shouting "Here's another one who has got to do what he's told by a slag. Well you can fuck off Exley, we don't need you anymore."

As Billy went to go Ronnie got hold of him by the throat and said, "You haven't seen anything, have you? And if any of this gets out, your fucking life won't be worth living." With that they let Billy go.

When I met Billy a couple of days later, he told me what had taken place. I really and truly felt so sorry for him, as I should know what it is like to suffer at the hands of the Krays. Billy was such a nice man, one you would not associate with being on the Krays firm. All Billy kept saying to me was "Lenny, I wish I had never met those two wicked, evil bastards. I only wish that I could walk away from them because the both of them are stark raving mad."

I know that Billy really liked Frances and so did a lot of people in the East End, but who was to know what those two mad bastards would get up to next? Billy Exley was a good family man who loved his wife and kids. He was not on his own, there were others that were drawn into the firm. Once you were in, there was no way out. The only way anyone got off the firm was if the Krays had no more use for you.

My dear friend Billy Exley has sadly passed away now, along with Frances Shea. I call her Frances Shea as I don't want her name to be tarnished with the name Kray. She deserves much, much more than that. At least they are both out of the Krays' evil clutches.

To my very dear friends: God knows how much you both have suffered and He will look after you. God bless the both of you, you are now both at peace, away from their evil clutches. Don't worry, you have no chance of meeting them in the afterlife, because the pair of you are in heaven, and there is only one place those two evil bastards will have gone, and that is hell.

In 1968, some people did have the courage to speak out

and bring the Kray's empire crashing down. Even some of the firm turned against the twins and gave evidence against them at the Old Bailey. There were some villains who phoned up Nipper Read to give information about the Krays even though some of these men refused to stand in the dock. In a way I can't say that I blame them.

But I say good luck to those who did give evidence against the Krays.

It is now more than 30 years since the Krays received their sentences at the Old Bailey and a lot of the old East Enders have since died.

Ronnie Kray died in hospital after he was taken there from Broadmoor.

Reggie was released from prison on compassionate grounds, but died shortly after from cancer. His funeral took place on 11th October 2000. Charlie has also died.

And I don't think that Reggie did himself any favours by giving Ronnie such a big send-off when he died. It was more like a Mafia send-off – but then Ronnie always did fancy himself as an Al Capone.

Of the many people who turned out to see his funeral, few went to show their respect. Most were only there out of sheer curiosity. Above all the noise of the crowd, I heard one woman's voice shout, "Murderer!"

There have been a lot of books written about the Krays, plus television programmes and even the film, The Krays. The film was in very poor taste in its depiction of their dear old mum, Violet, and dear Aunty May whom they loved so much. In real life they were the opposite of how they were portrayed in this film. I shouldn't think the Krays were very pleased with that aspect of the film either.

When Justice Melford Stevenson read out the Kray twins' sentence at the end of the long Old Bailey trial, he gave them life terms — quite rightly so — and recommended that they were both to serve at least 30 years. I pray to God that the present and future generations will never have to experience the likes of the Krays ever again.

In the 1960s people used to say that the Krays must have come from hell. I should imagine that that is where the pair of them have found their last resting-place. And it couldn't happen to two nicer people, could it? We all say in the East End that they finally got their comeuppance.

glossary

Bird - To do bird is to spend time in prison

Foolery - Jewellery

Jar - Pint

Jump-up - Steal an already-loaded lorry

Manor - Area

Peter - The cell that is allocated to you

Spielers - Illegal clubs where people play cards

Suited/booted - Smartly dressed

Tanner - Sixpence (old coin) worth 2½ p in today's money

Telephone numbers - To speak the Queen's English

Tickle - Robbery

Tom - Tom Foolery, as in jewellery

Trot - Absent without leave (AWOL)

Twirls - A set of keys

VO - Visiting Order

addendum

Before I was a witness on the Kray trial against Ronnie Kray for burning me with those red hot pokers in 1961, I stood by and respected the code whereby, no matter what happens, the one thing you did not do was 'grass'. I stood by that code until 1968 – that was the year the Kray twins threatened to shoot my two children. I then signed a statement in the presence of Leonard 'Nipper' Read, the main officer in charge of the Kray case, in return for police protection for my two children.

It is so easy for people to call me a grass without knowing the full meaning of the word. In my own way, I will try to explain the full meaning of the word 'grass'.

In the old days a grass was a whisperer, originating from

the wind blowing through the tall grass, making it 'whisper'. Therefore, the phrase 'whispering grass' was formed.

In the criminal world a grass is scum and I would go along with that. In the old days if they found out who a grass was, they would scar his face with a cut-throat razor, but that has all changed.

There are now different types of grass. One type of grass is a paid police informer, and is protected by them. A second type of grass is a person who would turn Queen's evidence to save his or her own skin in a criminal case. Another type is called a 'supergrass'. These are people who do not care who knows their identity and will be hiding for the rest of their lives. They have to change their names and move to different parts of the country, even moving abroad to live. For the rest of their lives they will always be looking over their shoulders.

I put my life on the line by going on the Kray case, and I admit that I do not have any feelings of guilt at all in going to trial. I would do it all over again if anyone threatened my family. I also admire anyone put in the same situation as me, who does the same as I did.

I can be threatened, burnt with pokers or whatever, but don't, and I mean don't ever, ever threaten my family, because they mean everything to me.

The East End was once a very tight-knit community, but not any more. The old cockneys are a dying race, and most of the humour has departed with them. Today you have people from all walks of life moving into the area. We old cockneys have to learn to live with that. We have all got to live together. There are good and bad people everywhere, and it is the bad people that make life harder for the good.

I must admit that I was really scared of the Krays for a long time and so were many others, but I am not any more. I am an old man now. Over the past sixteen years I have had a good life, and I do feel sorry for a lot of people with hardships that they have had to endure. But those two wicked people deserved all they got.

As you can see by reading this true story, I have been no angel in my earlier days. I do not kid people and I'm not here to give you any false impressions of myself, only the truth. Unlike Reggie Kray, I do not have to manipulate people, or try to make them think that I am somebody I am not. When I saw Reggie on a television programme kissing two little choir boys in church, it made my flesh crawl. That was only done to try and fool the public into thinking that he can't be such a bad person. I could understand it if it was his brother Ronnie doing that because he was the one that liked young boys. I knew the Krays for over fifty years and have witnessed such things with my own eyes so I know exactly what they were capable of doing to people, be they villains or not. I am only one of the many people that have suffered at the hand of the Krays. I have known quite a few villains in my time and some I have the utmost respect for, but not the Krays. After reading several books about them, I have to admit I have changed my mind and am glad they stayed where they did. Nobody gave them the right to be judge and jury.

Lenny Hamilton

I was just a kid in the thirties. If you had a fight with someone, no matter if you won or lost, you would both shake hands afterwards, and you would still have respect for each other. That was the only way of life in the real East End.

To be honest, Ronnie and Reggie were natural-born gangsters and killers. They lived well and dressed well, but so could we with other people's money. Reggie was the brains behind all their evil deeds. Ronnie was just insane, and Charlie — well, he had to do as he was told.

In the end, let us not forget all the people that suffered at their hands, whether they were beaten, slashed, maimed or murdered, and thank God for the true stars of our country, who commit themselves to caring for the sick and disabled.

AN ODE TO THE BROTHERS GRIM

DOING THE BIZ

We know that we are here for a long stay
Thirty long years because we are Kray
Me and me twin, we got a rough deal
For the two villains that we did kill

There is only one thing that I can say
Yes it is true, Ronnie is gay
While we are here, we will make no noise
If you promise that Ronnie gets little boys

We ruled the East End, and the West
Being twins, we thought we knew best
Just goes to show how wrong you can be
Because me and me twin are in prison you see

We never hurt anyone, only our own
Just goes to show how the Kray firm has grown
We cut them, we shot them and stabbed them to death
Made sure that two bodies were never left

Lenny Hamilton

We ran all the rackets, protection that is
And showed everybody, how we did the Biz
The trouble we caused no one can tell
Yes it is true, we're the Kray twins from hell

Ron, he was barmy, but me I am sane
How people trembled, when you mentioned our name
Fear is the worst thing that people can't take
For it was we, the twins, that decided your fate

Ron, he lured a young man to his club up west
Had some of the firm there, at his request
He burnt him with pokers, done him real bad
That goes to prove that Ronnie was mad

Ronnie was a sadist, liked seeing you squirm
That's why the Colonel was head of the firm
He liked seeing you suffer, to inflict on you pain
Now he's in Broadmoor, for the criminally insane

He liked to let people think he was generous and good
But take it from me, he was no Robin Hood
He robbed everybody, the rich and the poor
Like Oliver Twist, he kept wanting some more

334

Branded by Ronnie Kray

He helped the old people and kids so they say
But never to mention that Ronnie was gay
He shot George Cornell because he called him a queer
And because of that, George paid very dear

Poor Jack the Hat, Reggie stabbed him to death
Then slit his throat, to make sure he was dead
He told Ronnie Bender to get rid of the corpse
Until this day he has shown no remorse

Frank Mitchell, they sprung him from jail
They made him think that he was their pal
He trusted them dearly and look what he got
Taken outside and finally shot

There was Terry asleep in his bed
Woken up by the Krays, who ripped his body to shreds
They stabbed him, they cut him like two evil witches
Terry wound up having three hundred and seventeen stitches

They mixed with the rich and famous at times
Even though they committed the most terrible of crimes
They liked their photos taken with the famous that is
It's what they meant by doing the Biz

Lenny Hamilton

Chris Lambrianou got fifteen years bird
He was totally innocent of the murder, we had heard
If the Krays told the truth he would have only got three
But Ronnie said – No, it's not gonna help me

Poor Ronnie Bender, I like him a lot
Twenty long years, that's what he got
For keeping his mouth shut, has done him no good
For they've slagged him off as much as they could

Nipper Read who they feared the most
They couldn't buy him
He wanted them in jail
The two brothers Grim

Ronnie has gone now, from this world of ours
When he got buried there were plenty of flowers
He did most of his time in the nut house that is
Is that what they meant by doing the Biz

Time is a good healer, so people say
So let's not forget those evil brothers called Kray
They have hurt loads of people many times
And now they are paying for their evil crimes.